INDEX

1st Printed August 2005

Printed by:
ROWE THE PRINTERS
Imperial Works
Guildford Road Industrial Estate
Hayle, Cornwall
TR27 4PZ

ISBN No. 0-9552152-0-X

Published by :-

Deane's Publications
20, Fountain Court
St. Clare St.
PENZANCE
Cornwall U.K.
TR18 2PT
Tel: 01736 360602

e-mail: deane.wynne@btinternet.com

ILLUSTRATIONS

****

Joseph Stalin

Saddam Hussein

Emperor Hirohito

Hitler & Mussolini

"Men of Power"

What can we do friends, you and I, to rid this world of ill?
We fought two wars for worldly peace so no more would men kill!
But still our world is full of strife in almost every sphere,
For there are men of 'evil mind' who want OUR lives to steer !

How come that single men as these can rally many others
To escalate their bad intent to detriment of brothers?
Minorities around the world 'sound off' quite loud and clear.
It seems to me the rest of us all 'listen' with deaf ear!

They say "Like Lions" we should be. But like all wildlife, game,
They fight for dominance of herd and we do just the same!
The sad part of this system is, that 'temporary' power,
Is all the winner really gets in this, "His finest hour"!

For there is always someone else, awaiting in the wings,
To wrest that power from the top and all that power brings.
Meanwhile, mere mortals, such as I, are 'fodder' for these men.
To be put down if we should dare to question from our den.

I have no answer to assuage these troubled times, this hell.
Like most I live my mortal life cocooned within my shell.
I try to live within my means, give no one any trouble.
My only wish? These "Men of Power" would live in their own 'bubble'!!!

Deane Wynne

DEDICATION

This book is dedicated to my late wife and sadly missed soul mate Maureen who interminably suffered my war stories over the years.

Also to my children Richard and Jacqueline, and my stepsons Tony and David. Not having lived in those harrowing years I cannot expect them to realise that there ARE times when the stupidity of war becomes inevitable!

They would never willingly fight in another war and I would not blame them for that. But I ask myself, what would they do if a tyrant was about to overrun their country?

I must not leave out my delightful grand children! Lee, Angela, Michael, Sian, Heidi and Lucas and make mention here that, had I not been fortunate enough to survive the war, neither my own children nor their offspring would be here today! Such is fate! I particularly worry for them in this troubled and uncertain world.

I also dedicate my story to the memory of the 35,000 (One in four) Merchant Seamen who gave their lives, more often than not in the most lonely and horrible circumstances, in their great endeavour to keep the vital supplies of Food, Oil, Petrol and Arms flowing into our tiny Island Kingdom. Without their stalwart dedication to duty this country would undoubtedly have succumbed to the evil tyrany it became our job to destroy, and succumb we very nearly did!

The men who crewed these ships often lived in very poor conditions and were often poorly fed. Their wages were stopped the minute their ship was sunk!

A derisory pittance of about £20 was paid in compensation for the loss of all their personal belongings. They had to kit themselves for sea again from this.

PROLOGUE

In this book I have attempted to record the feelings and experiences of a 17 year old going to sea "Below the Mast" at the beginning of 1942 in wartime. My story is written from memory some 57 years later.(My life has always been too busy to write it before, and I did not have the aid of a modern computer!) Apologies are therefore offered for any inaccuracies that might occur. I would assure the reader though that all I have written is vividly pictured in my mind still, and there are instances where I have taken advantage of other authors' researches to jog my memory.

The book is a record of the hard life lived and worked below decks on a typical pre-war Tramp Steamer.The coal burning ss.Veni in particular. She was built by Austin & Pickersgill Ltd., in Sunderland in 1901 and was still sailing the turbulent waters of the North Atlantic during the war but now under the Norwegian flag.

My reminiscences also cover some very rough crossings of the North Atlantic in both Cargo ships and Ocean going Rescue Tugs. All these voyages were in slow convoys often taking as long as 21 days each way. Hurricanes and the U-Boat menace constantly threatening us. My own torpedoeing at midnight on St.Patrick's Day, March 17th.1943 will never be forgotten!

The Normandy invasion was another never to be forgotten experience. I was aboard the large Rescue Tug H.M.R.T. Samsonia at the time. We towed an old French battleship the 'Courbet' over to Ouistreham where we blew the bottom out of her, sinking her to deck level to form part of the 'Gooseberry' breakwater for the Mulberry Harbour. We then towed many of the 7,000 ton concrete caissons known as 'Phoenixs' over for the Mulberry Harbour itself.

I left Samsonia a couple of months after D-Day and was transferred to H.M.R.T. Assiduous where many more adventures were to befall me on our way out to the far east where I remained until the end of the war with Japan.

I hope the reader may find my adventures interesting? Particularly any Deep Sea Tug men. I have seen nothing written about the hard, and often dangerous situations faced by our Deep Sea Tugs during the war. About 20 of them were lost at sea. Often with all hands. Some were sunk by enemy action, others foundered in heavy seas.

I only wish I had the expertise, experience and wherewithal to research Admiralty Records and write a full and true account of their many deeds of bravery!

GOD BLESS THEM ALL

AN INTRODUCTION

"Now....the day war broke out!"

This infamous day occurred just 15 days before my 15th Birthday. I remember it well in spite of the 59 years that have elapsed since I write.

I was living with my widowed Mother at the top of a three story block of flats alongside the film studios at St. Margarets in Twickenham, one of the larger western suburbs of London. We both listened to Prime Minister Chamberlain's broadcast on that fateful Sunday morning of September 3rd 1939. His declaration of War against Germany sent a cold shiver through us both. The fact that the air raid sirens mournful wail sounded off only minutes later did nothing to calm our fears as to what the future held! I don't know what we expected to see when we looked out of our windows: Masses of Bombers? Bombs dropping everywhere? If they were we were standing in a very vulnerable place by the window! In the event, the only thing in sight was a rather portly Air Raid Warden riding around on his bicycle. He wore a tin helmet and an arm band with ARW written on it proclaiming his status. He was blowing furiously on his whistle. We stayed where we were. No point in panicking! Eventually the All Clear sounded , it had been a false alarm. The milkman in the background of the picture is obviously more concerned to get his milk delivered regardless of what the enemy might do!

A tin hatted Air Raid Warden takes a break for a mug of tea at his post. Air Raid Wardens were the linchpin at local level of the British Civil Defence System. Each post was supposed to control an area of about 500 people. In London there were about 10 posts to the square mile. In 1939 there were 1.5 million Civil Defence personnel, over two thirds of them volunteers.

Mother of course, with vivid memories of the Great War and the hundreds of badly wounded men she had helped to nurse in hospital, was immediately fearful for her only son's future. As young as I was, I tried to allay her fears. After all, I WAS the man of the house! We discussed what needed to be blast. Black out curtains were needed. Candles against power cuts. A few tins of food as emergency stock. This proved a little difficult as panic buying of tinned food and dried goods had quickly denuded the shops. However, we did manage to get hold of a few modest items.

Monday morning found everyone going off to work as usual. Mother to the 'exclusive' Mayfair hairdressing salon where she had been the Receptionist and Manageress for the last 12 years; myself to the engineering factory in Chiswick where I was in the first year of my apprenticeship.

I don't think many minds were on the job that day! Everyone seemed to have their own opinions about what would happen and what the outcome would be. The routine soon settled back to normal though. Very little seemed to have changed. Eventually everyone had to register for an Identity Card. Gas masks were issued in little brown carrying boxes.

The entrepreneurs soon designed a range of more sophisticated carrying cases and no doubt a few fortunes were made from them! Food rationing was instituted and life started to become a little harder as Freedom of Choice was eroded in many areas.

Men queuing up for tickets at a Cinema carrying their gas masks with them

Dominoes and gas masks in a London family's Anderson shelter. A corrugated iron construction sunk into 1,000's of back gardens. These shelters were to save many lives during the Blitz.

Inside it felt a bit like being entombed in a small, dark bicycle shed, smelling of earth and damp.

My company decided to form it's own LDV (Local Defence Volunteers) force, the forerunner of the Home Guard (Dad's Army). Being a member of my local army cadet corps and the proud possessor of a uniform. I thought I should join. We held parades after work in the evenings. Fire watching rosters were organised and I found myself spending a couple of nights a week on the factory roof armed with nothing more than a stirrup pump and a bucket of sand in case incendiary bombs landed on us. This was an unpaid chore of course and, until the air raids really got started some months later, these nights, especially in winter, became very monotonous and tiring.

A Heinkel HE 111 drones over the East End of London in a daylight raid. This dramatic photograph was distributed throughout Germany to suggest how vulnerable the Capital of the British Empire was to Hitler's bombers.

By now I had found life at the factory had become boring. I had progressed from sweeping the floors and running errands at the start of my apprenticeship, and was now a machinist operating a centre lathe. My days were spent turning out small precision parts for the naval gun sights my company manufactured. We worked to tolerances of 1/10,000th of an inch.

All jobs were given a time limit by the Time & Motion Study Engineers so there was no time for idle gossip with your mates! While busily turning out these small repetitive parts on my lathe, my mind used to wander to what seemed to be a much more glamorous and exciting life beyond the factory gates!

Air raids were by now a frequent occurrence, often by day as well as night. I think my turning point came one day during a daylight raid when I actually watched a stick of bombs leave a German plane. I followed them down with my eyes, mesmerised, until I heard them explode, one after another only two or three streets away. I wondered what poor so and so's had just departed this world from that lot!

I decided there and then that this was not for me. I did not fancy just standing around while the enemy dropped bombs on me. The euphoria of war was gaining momentum and many were joining the forces. I decided I wanted to be in it. I wanted the chance to fight back in some way.

I was a gangling 6' tall and just turned 16 years old. I was proficient at foot and rifle drill through my time with the Army Cadet Corps. If I was going to be a soldier nothing short of an elite Guards Regiment would be my goal. With this in mind, and unbeknown to my Mother, I took a bus up to Whitehall in London one Saturday morning, I walked into the Recruiting office there and was confronted by the most magnificent and awe inspiring man I had ever seen. He was at least 6'6" tall. This Guards Recruiting Sergeant sported a thick snowy white head of hair with a fully waxed handlebar moustache to match. The sleeves of his blue uniform tunic were covered in gold embroidered badges and crossed flags. Two rows of medals adorned his chest. As a 16 year old I just stood and gaped at him in total awe! Suddenly his stentorian voice shook me from my reverie. "What can I do for you lad?" I almost trembled when I heard him. "I've come to join the Guards, Sir" I stuttered. I recall him looking me up and down with a critical eye before breaking out in a beaming smile. "That is very noble of you laddie, a very wise choice the Guards. We would be most honoured to have you I am sure, when you are old enough. "But I am sir, I am 18". I would very much doubt that laddie. Have you got your Birth Certificate with you?" I hadn't. I didn't even know where Mother kept it. He gave me a sort of Fatherly smile as he said "Well come back when you have it. Cheery bye for now.". My ego had been completely shattered and I was quite crestfallen!

On the bus journey home I considered my next move! The Merchant Navy I thought! There is no age barrier there, and promptly laid my plans in that direction.

I realised that my Indentures as an Apprentice Toolmaker were a binding contract and I would have great difficulty in getting out of them, so I went back to work for a few months but acted very indifferently to my tutors and deliberately made a bit of a mess of a few jobs I was given. I also let it be known that I did not think I was suited to this type of work. I managed to stick it out until January 1942 though. I was now 17 and made a determined effort to get to sea, hopefully as some sort of Junior Engineer. I was totally ignorant of what I was getting into and I was to find out that it was a world alien to me. I had no Father to guide me, having lost him when I was 18 months old so all I ever did in life was find my own way, usually the hard way, but I had a good boarding school education behind me and had learnt how to fend for myself.

The start of 1942 was a time for new resolutions to be made, and 'positive action' to be determined. I took a Monday off work and a bus to London to start making calls on the various shipping offices in Leadenhall St. I visited quite a few with no success, but at least was asked to leave my name and address in some of them. I was not too despondent therefore and went home to await results. I did not have to wait long. On the Thursday of the same week I received a Telegram asking me to report to the Dutch shipping offices the next morning. I duly turned up before they even opened, and when they did I had to wait a further hour before being ushered into a Manager's office.

I was offered a job as an Officers Steward on the Dutch Cargo ship ss. Hilversum providing I could join her that very evening in Immingham Docks, Hull. I was hoping to get into Engineering and tried not to show my disappointment. As I was keen to get away to sea however I thought I MUST take this job to get me started in the Merchant Navy. I accepted the offer therefore, and was handed a railway warrant and Boarding Pass and wished "Good Luck".

Mother had helped me draft a letter to my employers the night before and I phoned her at work and asked her to post it, at the same time informing her of my success and movements. Then I was away to catch the train to Hull. The journey seemed to take an eternity. Hull was further north than I had imagined. My mind wandered all over the place during this journey! I wondered where my first ship would take me. Thoughts of the dangers to be faced never crossed my young mind!

ss.HILVERSUM
(My first ship and very nearly my last)

I eventually arrived in Hull during the late evening black out. Not having a clue where to go I would have to spend a large part of my meagre resources on a Taxi. I was anxious to find the ship and get aboard without any 'hassle' as I was now feeling very tired and a little apprehensive!

The Taxi was not allowed through the Dock Gates so I had a long walk in the black out to find the "Hilversum". I was not sure exactly what I was looking for but eventually had a little bit of luck when I noticed the letters SUM on the stern of a ship by dint of the small amount of moonlight. Closer examination revealed "Hilversum, Rotterdam" around her stern. She looked huge to me. With no cargo she stood very high in the water and her gangplank was almost vertical to walk up. My arrival on deck was greeted with a deadly hush. There was no one in sight. My tentative calls of "Anyone aboard" eventually brought the night watchman out from the 'fiddley top' where he had been enjoying a warm and a quiet smoke. He spoke to me in Dutch which was quite incomprehensible!

I showed him my boarding pass and then, beckoning, said "Kom" and took me through to the saloon and called the Chief Steward who appeared to be enjoying a good drinking session with the ships officers. At least HE spoke some English and told the night watchman to take me 'aft to the crews quarters'.

Apart from the hum of the ships generator and the slow 'whine' of what turned out to be the Weir boiler feed pump the ship seemed to be very quiet. The crew were all ashore but there was a coffee pot simmering away on the upright coal 'bogey' that also served to heat the quarters. The watchman showed me my bunk and indicated I should sort myself out before the crew returned aboard. By now I was almost asleep on my feet. The train journey, especially the last couple of hours in the black out was tedious to say the least. I dearly wanted to turn in but thought I had better wait up for the rest of the crew. If they returned and found a stranger sleeping in one of their bunks they may well have wondered who I was!

I did not have long to wait before I heard the sounds of some unfamiliar singing coming from the quayside. The 'noise' got progressively louder as the crew tumbled aboard. From what had obviously been a very heavy nights drinking! One by one they collapsed on the seats either side of the mess room table. The coffee pot spilled a fair amount of its dark liquid content as it was unceremoniously thumped down on the table top. Yells of obscenities came from one unfortunate sailor who received some boiling hot coffee in his lap.

I was eventually noticed as an unfamiliar face. My replies to their enquiries elicited a few "Ah, English" from around the table. Most of them were so drunk they rather put the wind up me, being the young teetotaller that I was at that time! I decided the best thing to do was turn in my bunk and made my fumbled excuses the best way I could. I heard a couple of "Velderooster's" (Sleep well) the only Dutch word I ever learnt and remember to this day. I thought it rather quaint! There was little chance of any sleep with all the unintelligible chatter that was going on, but sleep I must have in the end. It seemed like only an hour before I was roughly shaken and told to get up to the saloon 'Pronto'. It was about 6 a.m. A quick sluice in cold water and a comb of my hair was all I had time for before I was shouted for again. I rushed up on deck and ran along to mid-ships where I saw the Chief Steward leaning over the bridge veranda looking for me. He briskly told me to clear the saloon of all the dirty plates, glasses and ash trays from last nights drinking session. "Then get the breakfast laid" he said.

The saloon stank of stale cigar and cigarette smoke, so the first thing I did was open all the portholes to try and ventilate the place. The Chief Steward, looking as though he had a hangover from the night before, seemed to have little patience with my ignorance of where to find or put things! This flustered me even more. However, with more than a little help from him all was eventually laid out to his satisfaction.

I was then told to go down to the galley and fetch the porridge. This was presented to me in a large China tureen which I had to carry along the main deck, up a slippery steel stairway to the lower bridge deck, and thence to the saloon. Guess what? I dropped it while climbing the stairway. A great start to my new career! The Chief was livid! I was berated in the most colourful of Dutch and English expletives. He managed to get some more porridge from the cook and took over the serving of the breakfast while I had the most difficult job of cleaning both, myself, the deck and the stairs of a tureen of hot sticky porridge. It occurred to me to wonder how I was going to be able to carry the food up to the saloon in rough, wet and windy weather!

We sailed after breakfast. For where? I knew not. We headed north from the Humber in a mixed convoy of coastal and deep sea ships. Destroyers, armed trawlers and a couple of M.L.'s escorted us.

The Chief spent all morning trying to educate me as to my duties and, I suspect, evaluate whether I would ever be likely to make it as a Steward or not!

I managed to get lunch up from the galley without mishap, also the evening meal which was served as we entered the river Tyne and proceeded upstream to the coaling berth at Dunstan.

Part of an east coast convoy with barrage balloons up. Most of them coal burning ships as can be noted from their tall funnels to catch the draught.

Sheer exhaustion allowed me to sleep well that night in spite of all the noises in the busy river. The next day though was to be horrendous. The ship was loading a full cargo of coal as well as bunkers. Everything you touched was covered in coal dust. The crockery, glasses, tables, chairs, our clothes, hair and shoes. The fine black dust penetrated everywhere It was even trodden into the saloon carpets. I could not keep on top of it and wept with frustration. At the end of an awful day I could not wait to get ashore and away from it all.

My run ashore brought little relief. I wandered around in the black out with little money in my pocket. Eventually sitting in a grubby little café near the docks where I washed down a couple of indifferent Rock Cakes with a mug of tea before finally returning aboard our coal dust laden ship.

My troubles were far from over though. I was sitting at the mess room table, minding my own business as I could not join in the general conversation anyway, when a big burly Dutchman sitting opposite me, obviously the worse for drink, suddenly picked up a table knife and threw it at me with some force. I did not have time to dodge it and it hit me squarely across the nose. The pain almost knocked me senseless and blood spurted everywhere. Other crew members restrained my assailant while another took me to the Chief Steward who also kept the medical cabinet. He decided I needed a Doctor and an ambulance was sent for. I spent the rest of the night in the casualty department of the local hospital where three stitches were put across the bridge of my nose which was then heavily plastered up. I was discharged from the hospital the next morning and had to find my own way back aboard feeling very sore and sorry for myself. The Captain held an enquiry which resulted in my assailant being fined two weeks pay. I was asked if I wanted to continue aboard and quickly decided my experiences of the last two days were more than I wanted to continue with. I felt there was little future for me, the only Englishman aboard this Dutch ship and took the opportunity to leave her there and then The Captain was kind enough to give me the two weeks pay he had fined my assailant.

Mother of course, was surprised to see me home again so soon! She was also surprised to see my heavily plastered nose. I was quick to assure her the Germans had nothing to do with it before relating the sorry story. A few days later I visited my local hospital where they removed the stitches. I was told nothing could be done about the broken bone and as it was no longer painful resigned myself to it.

By now I had plenty of time to reflect on my unfortunate situation! I had already decided that 'one bad egg' could not allow me to give in so easily and I would try to find another ship, albeit giving the Dutch a wide berth and definitely not taking on another stewards' job again!

I did the rounds of the shipping offices in Leadenhall St. once more. Someone told me to try the Norwegian Consul in Tavistock Square. I took the hint and a bus there. I told the shipping manager that I had just signed off the "Hilversum" and was looking for a berth as a Junior Engineer, making no mention of the fact that I had been a steward for two days only. I was asked to wait as something may be available shortly. I hung about for the rest of the morning and was asked to return after lunch. This looked promising so I did.

A mug of tea and a corned beef sandwich in a nearby café sufficed for lunch while I pondered my chances. On returning after lunch I was immediately ushered into the Manager's office. "Could I make my way to Southampton this afternoon?" I was asked. We have a ship there the ss. "Veni". What is the job?" I asked. "Oh, You can become a Junior Engineer" he replied. I was excited and accepted. He gave me a rail warrant and boarding pass.

For my part I was probably a little over profuse in my thanks! It never occurred to me why he had not asked for proof of my previous experience! I hoped I would find the Norwegians a little more friendly than the Dutch!

A quick rush home for my gear, a phone call to Mother at work, and I was away to Waterloo Station to catch a train to Southampton.

CHAPTER TWO

ss.Veni

(A tramp ship if there ever was one!)

Built by Austin & Pickersgill, Sunderland in 1901-
Wrecked west coast of Scotland January 1st. 1946

The uneventful train journey to Southampton finally came to an end. I took a taxi from the Central Station to the main dock gate and showed my boarding pass to the dock yard policeman at the gate. He directed me to the Veni's berth. I lugged my suitcase for what seemed a mile on a very hot July day before I found her. It was then that my face dropped. Her rusting hull stood high in the water. The name 'Veni', Bergen was painted around her old fashioned counter stern confirming that this was the ship I had contracted to join. The 'Veni' was what is known as a 'three islander'. She had well decks between the fo'c'sle and bridge, and between the after end of the boat deck and the poop deck. Her straight and stubby bow ahead of her high fo'c'sle did nothing to enhance her lines. The high fo'c'sle head carried the anchor windlass on top. Underneath lay the seamens quarters, also the Bosun's locker where paint and deck spares were kept. Large wooden barrels containing Salt Beef, Pork or Herrings were lashed to the deck outside.

She had two cargo hatches in each well deck and a tall mast between each which carried her cargo handling derricks. A very tall 'Woodbine' funnel contributed to her ungainly lines but was very necessary to create the vast updraught needed to burn the coal in her natural draught boilers. The 'Hilversum' had at least been a well founded presentable looking ship by comparison. Albeit neither were up to the standards of the more modern flush-decked cruiser stern ships.

The Veni was only about 7,000 tons. She was launched as the 'Tonbridge' and sailed under the Red Ensign at the start of her life, eventually being sold to the Norwegians. She had been used in the Baltic timber trade or carrying Iron Ore from Narvik in Northern Norway to mainly German ports. Her Captain and crew had decided to make a run for England when their country was invaded by the Germans. We were of course, very glad to have her. Every ton of shipping we could get was desperately needed to replace the appalling losses we were suffering at the hands of the U-Boats.

I was to find out that the ' Veni', and many more like her that were well past there 'sell by dates' were to be at as much risk from the North Atlantic storms as they were from the U-Boats. Many of these ships would never have been allowed to sail in peacetime, but in war? Mens lives were of little account, let them sail and hope they will get through was the only criteria that mattered.

I reluctantly climbed her dirty gangway. On arrival at the top I was immediately smitten with an eyeful of ash blown from the large pile on deck. The ashes from the ships boilers and galley stove could not be dumped overboard until we were well out to sea. On top of the ash pile were vegetable peelings and all sorts of other galley waste that smelt to high heaven. I thought "Surely I cannot contemplate going to sea on a thing like this!".

I was obviously standing there looking a bit bewildered when I suddenly heard a voice speaking to me in a lilting Norwegian tone. I answered in English, which he immediately understood. I said "I am the new Junior Engineer". He seemed to raise his eyebrows a bit quizzically! "Follow me" he said and took me along to the Chief Engineer.

The Chief was busy with someone else at the time so, after a perfunctory introduction, he said to the sailor who had brought me along. "Ho,ho, take this man to the Chief Steward and get him fixed up in his quarters", to me he said "Come back and see me after lunch".

Ho,Ho! I thought. What a funny name. It turned out that his real name was Hans Hjalma Hansen and he came from a small town called Twedistan in the Norwegian Telemark District. The letter "H" is pronounced Ho in Norwegian, hence Hans nickname. We were to become very friendly on board. He was about my age and obviously missed his family in Norway very much. I often wonder whether he survived the war. I tried to trace him many years later while on holiday in Beautiful Norway, but to no avail. I found out many years later that the 'Veni' had been wrecked off the Scottish coast in 1946.

I found that most of the Norwegian crew called each other by the name of the town they came from. There was Oslo, Bergen, Tromso, Narvik, etc.

Ho,Ho, took me along to the Chief Steward who gave me a mattress cover and two dark grey blankets. He told me to come back after lunch for my rations. Rations, I thought! I did not know that we were rationed on board ship, but we were. A small amount of tea, sugar and butter per week also one tin of sweetened condensed milk. The only thing that lasted the week was the tea. The Norwegians preferred Coffee of which there seemed to be plenty. We used to punch two holes in the top of our milk tin and, as it was kept in the top of our locker and invariably handled with coal dust laden hands, you can imagine what it looked like after a couple of days. Mind you, coal is usually clean in spite of being black. Lots of old time stokers used to suck lumps of coal while stoking the boilers. Especially in the tropics. It stopped the mouth getting too dry in the heat

Ho,Ho then took me aft where I would be quartered with 'The black gang'(Stokers & Greasers)The black gang lived aft on most of the old tramp ships, while the seamen lived for'ard.
"You are the second Englishman we have on board" said Ho.Ho.We also have a Canadian. I was heartened to hear this and, on entering the mess deck was introduced to Peter Springham from Ware, in Hertfordshire. Pete was about my height and build and 3 months older than me. We got on very well together and were to remain firm friends for the next two years before finally losing touch with each other. Pete in turn, introduced me to Tom Casey the Canadian. Tom came from a small fishing village on the Northern tip of Prince Edward Island at the entrance to the great St. Lawrence river.

Tom had recently turned 18 so we were all much about the same age. He said he was the Lamp Trimmer. What on earth is a lamp Trimmer? I enquired. He pointed to the cause of the smokey 'fug' in the mess room. A Carbide duck lamp hanging over the table. The'Veni' had no generators.

All lights were Carbide, including the Navigation lights. Toms job was to ensure that the ships lights were primed and working efficiently at all times. The lights had smelly brown lumps of carbide in the bowl which, when water was added gave off a gas that was ignited.

I was to share a cabin with Pete. He of course, being the first on board had grabbed the lower bunk. He had only joined her a couple of days before me himself. "So you are the other coal trimmer?" Pete said. "Coal trimmer?" I replied. "I've joined as a Junior Engineer". He smiled. "They got you on that one too did they?" he said. We start at the bottom as coal trimmers, then progress through to Firemen, Greasers and Donkeymen. If, in the unlikely event you are still aboard this old rust bucket in a few years time, you might have a very faint chance of getting a fifth engineers job. You can't get any higher without you have completed an Apprenticeship, got some sea time in, and obtained your "ticket". Another big blow to my machinations!

I was already more than disenchanted with my surroundings but had taken an instant liking to Pete and Tom. I had signed on the ship 'For better or worse' and had no alternative employment so decided I must try and stick it out. I noticed some wooden slats across my bunk and said to Pete. "Where's the mattress?" Oh! That's what the mattress cover is for "he said. " I will take you down to the 'tween deck where there is a pile of straw you can fill it with". To me this was the ultimate primitive pit! What had I come down to? We went down into the gloomy, duck lamp lit 'tween deck. Pete told me to stuff as much of the straw as I could into the mattress cover. He said it soons breaks down and thins out so, if you don't really cram it in you will soon find you feel the wooden boards through it when you try to sleep. He helped me make what turned out to be a large round cylinder of straw, known as a Paliasse. My first three nights trying to sleep on this monstrosity were 'uncomfortable' to say the least! However, once it finally shaped down to my body size I found it to be very warm and comfortable. In any event, the work I was to do was so exhausting that I could have slept anywhere when I came off watch. Indeed there were many occasions when I just collapsed on top of a pile of coal in the bunkers and just slept until it was time to go on watch again.

By the time we had filled my paliasse and got it back to the cabin it was time for lunch. I followed Pete and Tom to the galley amidships. It was always our job to collect the food. The cook had the top half of the split steel door open. His galley looked a complete shambles to me. A large coal range along the after bulkhead on top of which were an assortment of large, well blackened, cast iron saucepans and dixies. The tiled floor was covered with ashes from the fire and grease from the food. His 'apology' for an apron was filthy. He handed Pete and Tom a large Dixie each which they carried aft to our quarters. I was handed a tray of small loaves of bread. We had to carry this lot down a steel ladder, across the well deck, and up another ladder to the poop, then down some steep wooden stairs to our mess room. It was difficult enough to do this in harbour. I dare not think what it would be like at sea in rough weather.

The 'Black Gang' had all assembled round the mess room table for lunch. There were 13 of us living in the cramped quarters aft. Pete took the lid off the first Dixie and each man passed his chipped enamel plate along for a ladle full of Norwegian Sweet Soup. This was a watery concoction of various dried fruits which the Norwegians appeared to be very fond of. We had it with nearly every meal. I suspected that, because the dried fruits were cheap to buy and easy to store, this was the real reason for having it!

The main course was Salt beef in a vegetable stew. The meat was mostly great slithers of fat and very unappetising. Potatoes 'swam' in the stew. At sea the cook had the very devils own job of getting at the barrels under the fo'c'sle head in rough weather. He was often swamped, and lost the meat on his way back to the galley. The deck crew had an even worse job trying to get their food for'ard from the galley as huge waves swept over the ships bows. It was bad enough for us trying to get it aft. Many a meal was lost for all the crew when at sea in the North Atlantic storms. When this happened it was deemed to be 'hard Cheese'. We were lucky if we managed to scrounge a bit of extra bread or corned beef from the cook. We were ALWAYS hungry on the Veni!

Cheese was fairly plentiful aboard, but it was a very coarse brown goats cheese peculiar to the Norwegians. It was as rough as sandpaper on your tongue. When in port we spent most of our pay on food. The first call ashore would always be the nearest café . Sometimes nearly the whole crew could be found there at the same time. The café owners did well when we were in port. Next we would buy all the food we could take back aboard. In Canada and the U.S.A. of course , we had no problem with rationing. Food was plentiful and cheap. It was a different matter at home!

After a very meagre lunch (I just could not fancy what I saw in that Dixie!) I went along to keep my appointment with the Chief Engineer. A 'Kom' in response to my knock on his cabin door invited me to enter. I was most impressed. I found a reasonably sized cabin, well furnished in highly polished Mahogany. The Chief was sitting at his desk. Drawers under each pedestal, leather topping and highly polished brass handles. He swivelled round in his leather upholstered Captains chair as I entered. He greeted me warmly enough, explained my duties to me, and hoped I would be happy aboard. I said, "It appears that I will be no more than a coal trimmer? I was told I was joining as a Junior Engineer" He replied that "All Engineers must start at the bottom and thoroughly learn the job if they are to understand it" I reflected on this in later years and came to the conclusion that the hard work I endured did me no harm and did, in fact, give me a better understanding of what was involved in the power pack of a ship!

Having taken in the luxurious surroundings of the Chiefs cabin compared to my own squalid quarters, I vowed there and then that I would attain such heights as soon as possible. I did finish my sea going career some 12 years later as a fifth engineer and even made third, then second on coastal ships.

I drew my meagre rations from the Chief Steward and repaired back to my quarters aft. Pete and Tom were dressed for going ashore. "Nothing to do this afternoon" they said. "Want to come ashore with us?"."Why not?, I replied. We made for the nearest dockside café and had something like a meat pie with mushy peas, bread and margarine and a mug of tea.

Pete said "I noticed you unpacking your gear. You do not appear to have any suitable working clothes or boots?" I hadn't of course. I did not anticipate the type of work I would be doing! My companions came to a ship chandlers with me where I found I had just about enough money on me to buy a pair of dungaree trousers (Jeans today) at 10/6d (52p) a pair, and some army style boots at about the same price. A good job I got them. They were certainly needed where I was to work.

Having obtained the necessary items we decided to go to the pictures. I forget the film showing at the time. When we came out we were hungry again. We managed to find a Fish & Chip shop that did us proud. My shipmates were then ready for a pint of beer or two!) I had never touched beer in my life, or been into a pub for that matter. I felt a bit nervous of going into the pub with them. In any event I had no money left, and told them so. "Oh! Come on in" They both said "We'll treat you."

At their insistence I went into the Dolphin Hotel just below the Barr Gate in Southampton where I had my first ever ½ pint of beer. I took a tentative sip and tried my best not to show the repugnance I felt at the taste of it. To me it was just like some foul medicine. Pete and Tom soon downed their pints and banged their glasses down on the counter for another. It did not take me long to become accustomed to the taste though and, by the end of the evening I found myself being propelled back aboard by my shipmates. We were all singing our hearts out. I flopped on to my prickly straw paliasse and just about died for the rest of the night.

The next morning Pete took me down below to show me around. We went down through the 'fiddley' door over the stokehold. The smell of steamy wet ashes, oil, and the heat that arose from below had to be got used to! There was a small steam operated winch on the 'fiddley' top. This was used to haul up the heavy steel buckets of hot steaming ashes, through the ventilators. It would be my job when on watch to empty these buckets over the ships side. About 30 steamy and very heavy buckets of wet ash had to be pulled out from a rectangular hole in the side of the ventilator. I would then have to carry the bucket a short distance to the ships side and tip the contents down a chute. This was no joke in foul, freezing and very rough weather. Especially at night. No lights could be shown anywhere on deck during the war. U-Boat Commanders have said they could even see someone lighting a cigarette through their periscopes.

We climbed down the vertical steel ladder to the 'tween deck where the coal bunkers were stored. In the gloom of the duck lamp I could just see some coal at one end. There was a large square hatch which led down to the boiler room. The coal had to be pushed along the steel deck in a large, and very heavy, steel wheelbarrow, then tipped down the hatch. This was the devils own job in rough weather. There was little enough light to see where you were going to start with. More often than not, having struggled to fill the wheelbarrow with coal, then staggered along the rolling deck with your load, you would lose balance and tip the lot over just before you got to the hatch.

It was exhausting and soul destroying work. You HAD to get the coal to the firemen somehow though. They would soon be howling at you if they ran out. Steam pressure HAD to be kept up at all costs so we could keep up with the convoy, and it all started with YOU! The sweat, the gloom, the heat, the backache. The coal dust in your eyes, your mouth, your hair, your ears, the pitching and rolling of the ship, all added up to an image of what hell must be like!

The Veni had two boilers. Massive 22 ft long Lancashires. Each had four furnaces burning coal by natural draught. The quality of the coal was of paramount importance to the stokers. Poor quality doubled their work effort (and mine) Welsh steam coal was always the best in the world.

The tools of their trade were energy consuming in themselves. The 'slice' or poker was a 2" diameter x 15ft. long steel rod flattened out at one end. Goodness knows what it weighed! It had to be handled with two thick sack cloths as it got red hot when pushed through the fire. It was used to lift the clinkered coals and aerate them, and to push them over to one side to get at the bottom clinker when cleaning the fires. The rake was similar in length but not quite so heavy. It had a half moon shaped blade at one end which was used to push or pull the coal to where it was most needed, and pull the old clinker out when cleaning the fires at the end of each watch.

The shovels were huge. To 'throw' a heavy shovel full of coal to the back end of the furnace was an art that had to be learned. You sort of banged the shovel on the dead plate at the front end of the furnace as you threw it. The coal then shot off right down to the back end. It was very important to be able to place the coal exactly where you wanted it so as to get the best combustion and heat for making steam. While you were doing all these operations of course, the furnace doors were wide open. The searing heat was burning your face and body as you worked. Your eyes were squinted up against the heat and glare. At the same time the ship might be rolling in heavy seas and shuddering strongly as a big wave hit the fo'c'sle head with a crashing bang.

Keeping a foothold on the slippery steel plates while working under these conditions was just another aspect of the stokers lot to be endured. If there was no wind up top to come down the ventilators it became almost intolerable. Not only was it much hotter, but the stokers had to work twice as hard as there was insufficient air to keep the coal burning brightly. More modern ships had forced draught boilers where large fans would provide the air to the furnaces. How so many of these old coal burners managed to keep station in convoy I do not know! From on deck there was no way of telling what the stokers were going through. On the other hand the deck crews had their own 'hell' from freezing seas!

When poor coal caused continual smoke to emit from the funnel, extremely irate messages would be flashed from the Commodore and Escorts. They never did seem to realise that the stokers were the very last people who wanted to give our position away to U-Boats by making smoke! They were much more vulnerable than anyone else if a torpedo should come through the thin steel plating of the engine or boiler room!

The Veni had what is known as a Triple Expansion Reciprocating Engine. It looked massive to me, but I was to sail with even bigger ones before I finally left the sea. The three huge pistons with their accompanying valve rods, were open to the engine room. It was fascinating to see them going up and down for hour after hour, day after day, without a stop. They would go on forever as long as the greasers ensured they were regularly splashed with lubricating oil and the bearings were well greased. The greasers arm went up and down in unison with the pistons as he flicked oil on to the guides with an expert hand. He had to put his hand right into the big ends as he felt them for temperature each time they revolved round. While performing these duties he always had to ensure that he had 'One hand for himself'. In rough seas he could easily slip on the oily steel plates and fall into the engine!

A long tunnel carried the propeller shaft to its ultimate end before it disappeared through the stern gland to the actual propeller on the other side. The steel shaft was about 15" in diameter and had many bearings along its length. Hard blocks of high temperature grease were put into a housing on top of each bearing. They had to be regularly checked and felt for overheating. The stern gland also had to be regularly checked for leaking.

No one liked going down the tunnel at sea. It was very gloomy with our carbide lamps. There was little head room and, in rough weather you could easily put your hand out to steady yourself and find you have placed it on the rapidly rotating shaft. The thoughts of a torpedo hitting the ship while you were in the tunnel did not bear thinking about!

Pete had the 8-12 watch. Morning and night of course. The other Norwegian Trimmer had the 4-8, so I was left with the 'Graveyard watch' 12-4. Having shown me around, Pete had to get on with some work. It was his watch. There were more ashes to get up and dump on deck. More coal had to be trimmed down to the stokers ready for sailing after lunch.

We sailed about 1 p.m. I had trimmed enough coal to the firemen in the last hour so was able to spend a little time on deck watching the activities of the harbour tugs as they edged us out of the dock and into the river Itchen. Clouds of thick black smoke emanated from our funnel as the banging and scraping of the firemens shovels could be heard working away below. The smoke blew down over the water and encompassed other ships still berthed alongside the quay, as we passed. They were very unhappy about this to say the least. I just stood nonchalantly on deck as if to say "It is nothing to do with me!" At the same time containing a certain amount of guilt within myself.

Once out into the river the tugs let go. The clang of the engine room telegraph and its reply to the bridge told me we were on our way. A big hiss of steam as the main engine turned, and the thrash of the propeller which was half out of the water, the ship being light, confirmed all was well and working.

I watched my surroundings and other ships we passed with great interest as we sailed down to Calshot Spit and the Solent. Pete came along and woke me from my reverie. "Don't you think you ought to get below and get some coal to them? It's better to take advantage of the calm waters while you can, especially when the bunkers are low. Once we get into the channel there will be at least a swell, and you will probably find that heavy wheelbarrow difficult to handle!" I took his advice and was able to move quite a bit of coal before I started to feel the gentle rock of the ship as we passed through the Needles and into the English Channel.

It was to be a very hard first watch for me. We had hardly got out into the Channel when I heard 'Bergen', one of the firemen, calling to me in the bunkers. "Lofty, Ve tak up de ashes now". As I was over 6' tall I got, and retained, the nickname "Lofty" throughout my sea going career. I climbed out of the bunkers and up to the fiddley top. Bergen said "Be sure you are knowing vat is de lee side?" I did. He then worked the steam winch as I nearly killed myself struggling to get those heavy steel buckets of hot, wet and steamy ashes, out through the ventilator and across the deck to the chute. About thirty buckets came up.

Once I had finished that I had to attack the huge pile of ashes and rubbish piled up on deck while the ship was in harbour. I then had to hose the deck down. I was absolutely exhausted and ached all over by the end of my watch when I was more than pleased to hand over to 'Narvik'. I had used muscles that I had never used before, and they let me know they did not take kindly to this sort of work! I envied those aboard Oil Burning and Diesel Engine ships who did not have any of this back breaking work or chores to do. I also wondered why I had not been lucky enough to find such a ship!

My watch over, it suddenly occurred to me! Where is the bathroom? I had not seen one anywhere! The reason being there wasn't one. I asked Pete. How on earth do we bath or shower?". "Behind the main engine "he said.

"You get a bucket of water, put an open ended steam jet from one of the pump drains into it, warm it up, then you'll find a wooden board behind the engine that you can stand on. Wash yourself all over with your sweat rag, that will clean it ready for use on your next watch. Then tip the bucket over you." I went back down below to do as he said. I found the firemen already there bathing so waited for them to finish. I must confess to being very embarrassed to start with. I had never bathed or showered 'in public' before!

We headed west down the Channel, joining a convoy that had come down through the Straits of Dover. A sleek looking Destroyer was among our escorts of armed trawlers and Motor Gun Boats. The wind was non-existent on this warm sunny day, and the sea flat calm.

The smoke from our funnel seemed to lay on top of the sea for ages as it slowly pulsed its way down over the ships side. We were the worst 'smoker' in the convoy. We eventually pulled into Dartmouth for the night. There is no finer scene than when entering this beautiful river with a blazing red sunset behind it. The narrow entrance to the tree lined slopes. The ancient town and the Britannia Royal naval College all add to its beauty and serenity!

I was thinking to myself, that's good we are anchored for the night. I will have nothing to do on my midnight watch! How wrong I was. I had to get those bunkers topped up with the next day's coal supply and, although there were not so many ashes to haul up, those that were had to be dumped on deck. I was very conscious of all the noise we were making during the night! I expect we were cursed by hundreds of people trying to sleep on other ships moored nearby and even the townsfolk ashore!

The convoy weighed anchor and sailed again soon after first light. We left the Channel again soon after lunch to go into Falmouth. We were to spend a few days there having a Great War 4.5" Howitzer fitted on our Poop deck aft. This would be right over my cabin. We all joked that we would probably sink ourselves rather than hit a U-Boat if we ever had to fire it in action!

It was a very hot summer day as we tied up to the quayside in Falmouth. Pete and Tom were ready to go ashore as soon as the gangway was down. I soon joined them. I clearly remember to this day that we ran all the way to the nearest Pub, lined up three pints of beer each, and drank them down non-stop. I guess Pete and I at least were partially dehydrated from our sweaty exertions on board.

We were certainly glad to enjoy a few days in Falmouth. There were always some chores to do in the morning but we had our afternoons off. Every day showed a clear blue sky and beautifully warm weather. We swam in the harbour and, as usual, went into town to eat. Usually Fish & Chips.

Welders from the dockyard came aboard and started making a large round steel platform over the Poop deck for the gun and its ammunition boxes. This was soon done and the arrival of the gun itself aroused much interest. The Able Seamen and Stokers were to be trained to fire the thing by a Royal navy Gunnery Petty Officer who sailed with us to Swansea, our next destination in South Wales.

Most of the training was done before we sailed, but then? The actual firing. We were in the Bristol Channel and had dropped back to the tail end of the convoy for this practice shoot. An empty oil drum was thrown over the stern, left to drift for some distance, then fired at. I was down below when the first shot was fired. The sudden tremendous bang had me running up on deck thinking we had been torpedoed. These 4.5"'s went off with a 'hell of a crack'. I think three shots were fired in all. No point in wasting ammunition. I don't think the oil drum came to any harm. It's probably still drifting around the oceans of the world somewhere! Anyway, that was the extent of our new armament and I don't think any of us felt any the safer for having it on board.

We went into Swansea for bunkers. Once again I was to be back among the coal dust. At least the 'tween deck was totally filled with coal, which meant we would have a few days of self-trimming when we sailed again.

We spent about a week in Swansea. The docks there were extremely dangerous at night in the blackout. Many a wartime sailor fell into them at night and drowned when walking back to his ship 'three sheets to the wind'. The docks were behind locks because of the tide in the river Severn. The water level was only just below the quayside. As the water was always covered with coal dust as well as the quay, it was almost impossible to differentiate between the two. Hence men stepped straight into the dock.

We finally left Swansea and headed up into the Irish Sea. We were bound for the River Clyde. We dropped our anchor among many other Merchant and Royal navy ships off Greenock. The Queen Mary was anchored quite close to us. It was the first time I had ever seen this magnificent ship. She looked huge, and she was. I felt I was almost aboard one of her lifeboats, so small were we in comparison. She was painted all over in her wartime grey but this did little to detract from her beauty. She was a regular visitor to the Clyde at that time while ferrying U.S. troops across the North Atlantic. I view of her speed of about 30 knots she was usually unescorted. There was one horrendous incident though that did not come to light until after the war. The light cruiser H.M.S. Curacao was in convoy with her. Apparently underestimating the Queen Mary's speed she cut across her bows. She was sliced in half and suffered great loss of life. The Queen Mary was said to have hardly felt the bump! She could not risk stopping to look for survivors as she would endanger herself and the 5,000 U.S. troops on board. It must have been a quick, but horrible end to have this great liner plough straight through you.

R.M.S. *Queen Mary* in her peace time livery

The day after we arrived in Greenock a small tender came out to us loaded with timber and a small army of Carpenters. We watched them encasing our chain steering gear that ran right along the deck, with a wooden box. I should mention here that the ships rudder was operated by a heavy steel chain that ran down from the bridge and along the after well deck to a large quadrant at the stern. I suppose you could say that we were a forerunner to power steering! It would have been impossible to turn the ships rudder without the assistance of a small steam powered winding gear. Once the chain had been totally boxed in, a barge full of sand arrived alongside. We hoisted this aboard in buckets with our own cargo derricks and spread it all over the well decks. This was meant to act as ballast for our forthcoming trip to Canada. We could no longer walk across the well deck, so a wooden catwalk was built across the hatches for this purpose.

A couple of days later we sailed in convoy down the Clyde. A vast assortment of merchant ships (most much more elegant than us!) escorted by Destroyers, a Corvette and an armed trawler. We all made our way in two lines until we reached the open sea, then we slowed down off Rathlin island, North of Ulster, while the escorts had the unenviable task of trying to get us into some sort of order. They appeared to be having quite a job. There were other ships that had joined up with us from Liverpool and the North of Scotland. The weather was quite rough and deteriorating fast.

A freezing cold Northerly gale soon came up from 'nowhere' and the Veni started to pitch and roll violently. The sand ballast soon had waves crashing over it, and a lot of it washed overboard. As darkness fell we had trouble steering the ship. It transpired that the sand had been washed through the cracks in the wooden casing surrounding the steering chain and jammed it. The wind worsened to Hurricane force. We soon lost the convoy and had no steerage way at all. ALL hands were called on deck and, roping ourselves to the nearest anchoring point we could find, we attempted to shovel the rest of the sand over the ships side. It was a struggle to keep your feet while the freezing waves crashed over you. We were in fear of our very lives as we drifted in the mountainous seas! We were not far from the very dangerous coast lines of Northern Ireland and the Scottish Islands. With no steering and the engines now stopped, we broached side on to the waves. With each roll from Port to Starboard we thought she would surely capsize! It became impossible to stay on deck, let alone shovel sand. The seas were now taking the sand away quicker than us anyway.

Down below in the engine room things were no better. The bilges were blocked with coal dust and filling up. The oily black water ran right up the ships side with each roll. In the boiler room large lumps of coal swished backwards and forwards across the ship in the rising water. The firemen had to climb up the ladders to avoid getting killed. We were losing steam fast. How on earth we survived that night I will never know. My first REAL trip to sea and this happens on my second day out! I have never been so frightened in all my life.

I remember, about two in the morning seeing a parachute flare lighting up the sky. It had been dropped by an aircraft. One of our gunners let fly with the Oerlikon gun on the boat deck, fortunately without success it was a Sunderland flying boat that had dropped down to investigate us. Our gunner thought it must have been a German. Eventually the rest of the sand was washed overboard. Once the decks were clear, the Bosun and Carpenter went along the deck with sledge hammers and broke away the rest of the wooden casing to free the steering chain. This was a heroic job in itself.

Almost totally exhausted, they were continually battered against the ships bulwarks or hatch combings as the mountainous waves still crashed over the side, nearly washing them overboard.

Fortunately there was still sufficient steam in the boilers to operate the steering windlass so, once the chain was free, the ship was tentatively brought round head to wind. This gave us some respite from the side rolling. Pitching was much more bearable and safer too. It was then ALL hands down below to help clear the bilges. The stokers were nearly waist high in water as they dipped in their shovels and tried to get enough dry coal to get some more life into the furnaces.

As dawn broke we detected a little easing off in the wind. Perhaps we were just in the eye of the hurricane! Anyway, steam was slowly raised again and we limped back into the Clyde. We were all totally exhausted but glad to be alive.

It speaks volumes for the designers and constructors of this old sea going warrior that the 'Veni' was able to stand up to such a battering 42 years after her launch! Such were Sunderland built ships in those days!

We were fortunate enough to spend the next week anchored off Greenock before another slow convoy would be formed for us to join. This time we carried no deck ballast at all but we would find we had other anomalies to cope with instead!

The day before we sailed again, a coal barge came alongside and we topped up with bunkers again. We trimmers had to stow the coal away in the 'tween decks which was hard and dusty work. However, it pleased us to know that we would not have to trim any coal to the firemen for the next few days after we sailed. And it would be a further week before we had anything like a long haul with the wheelbarrow.

We sailed again as before. A convoy of some sixty odd ships was brought into order off Rathlin Island by the escorts. Then we set off for Canada and the United States.

With only ashes to get up towards the end of my watch. I was able to stand in the warmth of the fiddley top and watch all the exciting things going on. It was a cold and windy day in September, 1942.

I was amazed to see the escort vessels shipping waves right over the whole ship. They were travelling a lot faster than us as they sped around the convoy. They were also, of course, very much smaller than us. I was certainly glad I was not on one of them! This weather though was nothing to what we were to meet further out in the North Atlantic. In fact the winter of 1942 was down on record as having had more violent storms than had been seen since records began.

It was only a couple of days before another hurricane hit the convoy. Having no ballast or cargo our propeller was only half submerged. As we dipped to each wave therefore, the prop .came completely out of the water causing the engine to race uncontrollably. If this were allowed to happen the big ends and tunnel bearings would melt in no time at all. Someone had to stand at the great throttle lever ALL the time. As the prop. came out of the water the lever was pushed forward to cut off steam and slow the engine right down. As the prop. bit into the sea again the lever was pulled back so forward propulsion could be maintained. Imagine doing this to every wave, for four hours at a stretch, for a whole week! At the same time trying to keep your feet on the slippery steel plates!

Our only consolation was that U-Boats could not attack us in such foul weather. However, we still got alarms that they were around !

We were about 13 days out of the Clyde before the weather started to ease off a bit. The convoy was behind its scheduled time due to the weather, and a few 'old timers' like us, not being able to keep up!

Although the wind had dropped considerably and the seas calmed to a long swell, our troubles were far from being over! We hit the dense fog that usually abounds over the Grand Banks off Newfoundland, especially at this time of the year. This meant that all ships were continually blowing their fog horns, including us. The mournful blasts went on day and night. It was amazing how much steam the fog horns used each time they blew! It made the stokers life that much harder in trying to keep steam pressure up.

Each ship trailed a Fog Buoy. Something like a five gallon oil drum on the end of a 200 ft rope. This enabled the ship behind to see if it was getting too close or not. It meant keeping a lookout in the bows to keep watching for the ship ahead's buoy There was continual whistling down from the Bridge to Engine Room to "Up 5 Revs, or down 5 Revs" To be among about 60 ships in dense fog is any captains nightmare. I think we spent 4 days in it on that occasion. Once out of it though, a new hazard arose! We were a sitting target for U-Boats. They liked to wait on the edge of the fog banks for us to emerge. Fortunately none bothered us on this trip.

The convoy started to split up soon after we cleared the fog banks Some ships went off to Starboard heading for St. Johns, Newfoundland. Others to Port for American cities. We carried on with quite a few others for Halifax, Nova Scotia. We were very thankful when we got into that magnificent harbour after 21 quite harrowing days at sea.

We entered the harbour at night. I was amazed to see the whole place lit up! I had not been used to lights at night since the beginning of the war. An added excitement for me was the fact that I had never visited another country before. We dropped anchor in the middle of the harbour which was 'alive' with ships of all types and nationalities.

The bustle of tugs and small ships everywhere, the unusual whistle of the Canadian trains ashore, these were all new sounds to me and held a certain fascination.

I hoped we would be allowed ashore the next day! The next morning we went alongside the coaling wharf to replenish our bunkers. The 'Veni' just 'ate'coal! Pete, Tom and I went ashore. Our first port of call? You guessed it. A 'diner'. What a meal we had. A massive 16 oz. 'T' Bone steak, with a complete mixed grill to go with it. An inch thick wedge of Apple Pie followed it, with Ice cream on top. Ice Cream? We only ever had this in summer at home. The Canadians and Americans had it all the year round and were obviously responsible for encouraging the habit in Britain after the war.

It did not take long to explore the town. Halifax is built on the side of a hill that runs along the left hand side of the harbour. The lower road is called Water Street.(What else?) This was mainly the home of Ship Chandlers, Repair Companies, Factories and Warehouses.

There was also a Seamans Club and Bar in Hollis St. which was more often than not the scene of much activity by the Royal Canadian Mounted Police. Albeit they were in cars rather than on horse back of course. It was only natural that sailors liked to enjoy a good drink to celebrate yet another successful crossing or inebriate oneself in readiness for the next!

There were no pubs in Nova Scotia. Drink could only be bought on Ration Cards, and from a Government owned Liquor Store for consumption at home or in a hotel if you were a resident. Higher up the hill and running parallel to Water St. was Barrington St. the main street and shopping centre of Halifax.

We settled for a bit of window shopping on this first run ashore but bought some groceries for aboard ship. Our priorities being fresh milk, bread and fruit.

The 'Green Lantern', Restaurant and Soda Fountain, a popular place with members of all the services in Halifax during the war.

The Allied merchant Seamans Club in Hollis St. Halifax.

Reading and relaxing inside the Merchant Navy Club. Would they be waiting for the bar to open I wonder? Note the Christmas decorations!

Having bunkered, we lost no time in sailing the next day. As we headed North after leaving the harbour we though we would be going down the St. Lawrence river to Montreal or Quebec! Wiser heads, however, said No. We would be iced in for the winter if we went there at this time of the year. They were right. We headed round the back of Nova Scotia and sailed up what appeared to be a Loch or Fjord. The water was flat calm. No wind blew at all. Our noisy propeller thrashed its way along toward our destination. Thick black smoke poured from our funnel and lay dreamily across the tranquil waters of this beautiful Loch. Forests of Fir Trees surrounded us on the shores. I thought "How nice it must be to live in such a place, far away from war torn Europe!"

Eventually we spotted a small township of typical wooden houses. A wooden jetty protruded out into the Loch.We moved in alongside it and were to remain there for three weeks while we loaded a cargo of sawn timber planks. Our arrival was quite amazing! Apparently we were the first foreign vessel to have visited this tiny port called Pictou since 1916. The village band was playing on the jetty. I think the whole town had turned out to join them. I could have wished for a better ship for them! Our old fashioned, rusty, smoke polluting hull did not seem to fit in with these beautiful surroundings somehow!

The local Mayor came aboard and offered a speech of welcome. The local 'Mounties' were also in attendance. No doubt wondering if this old tramp was likely to bring them any problems while here! The Customs Officer, no doubt also a local churchman, preached to us on the evils of drink and then proceeded to issue each man with a Ration Card to purchase it from the local Liquor Store. Each man was allowed to buy one bottle of whiskey or Spirits and ten bottles of beer a week. To be drunk ONLY on board! This was no problem for me, but my heavy drinking Norwegian friends did find it very frustrating. But, as always, there were ways round the Law providing you had the money. It did not take our crew long to find where extra supplies could be obtained!

Tom took the opportunity of our long stay in Pictou to go home and visit his family in Glace Bay, not so many miles away. Pete and I got rather bored with the place. There was nothing to do other than visit the only restaurant, really a Chinese Café with a couple of French Canadian waitresses. In the end we became a little more adventurous when we found we could take a train some twenty miles inland to a slightly larger town called New Glasgow. The train journey was a new experience in itself. It would suddenly stop in the middle of nowhere and pick up a milk churn or two that farmers had left by the side of the track. The odd country living person would also flag down the train if they wanted to go into town. Often there would not be a house in sight, let alone a station.

Half way to New Glasgow was a small town called Stellarton. It was just a little bigger than Pictou. For some reason the train stopped here for about two hours. We got off, wandered around killing time in the inevitable diner drinking tea or coffee.

New Glasgow itself was also a bit of a disappointment. At least there was a Cinema there but little to interest us otherwise. We went to the Cinema and found the film to be "Brief Encounter" under a different name. The third time I had seen it! By the time we got the train back to Pictou it was usually about 2 a.m. before we were back on board.

Once loaded we lost no time in sailing. The whole town turned out again to see us off. We were well replenished food wise and had bought plenty of fresh milk, bread, fruit and tinned stuff to keep us going for a few days at least. We had what looked like a hell of a cargo. It was stacked up on deck to bridge height. I remember thinking that no torpedo could sink us with this cargo aboard! Unless of course, he got a damn good shot right into the engine room and broke her in half!

Our three weeks in Pictou had tended to soften us up a bit and it was to be two or three days before we were back into our stride and became once more hardened to the hard and dirty work aboard.

It was only a short distance to our next anchorage. We went round the northern tip of Nova Scotia, through the Belle Isle Strait and dropped anchor off Sydney.

This was a very large safe anchorage which was used as a convoy forming up point during the war. I remember it being a cold, wet, and blustery evening as we lay at anchor for the night. There was much small ship activity as orders etc. were delivered round to the ships. A motor fishing vessel came alongside us. It was run by 'The Flying Angel' (Missions to Seamen) These wonderful people brought an assortment of hand knitted woollen garments aboard which they distributed free. There were Roll neck sweaters, socks, sea boot stockings, gloves and balaclavas, all knitted by the women of Canada for sailors. These items were particularly well received by the deck hands for the cold winter North Atlantic nights. Books, sweets and toiletries were also given to us. What a wonderful job these people do all over the world! They still do it to this day. The Padre of the Mission said a few prayers for us and left to go aboard yet another ship.

We sailed early next morning. The convoy quickly formed up, and we soon settled down to life aboard in the rough seas of the North Atlantic once more.

A couple of days out we joined up with another large convoy coming up from the south. This made us a combined force of about 70-80 ships if we included the escorts. We also had an Ocean going tug with us in case a ship was torpedoed and did not sink, or got into other difficulties. In this event the tug would try and tow it into the nearest port.

The seas were rough enough on our own ship, but when I watched the antics of the Tug, Corvettes and a Trawler as they 'corkscrewed' their way along, sometimes completely disappearing in the trough of some huge wave, I felt thankful I had something just a little bigger under me! How on earth these chaps lived, worked, cooked, ate, slept or even moved about doing their job on deck I found it hard to imagine! Later on, as the reader will discover, I was to sail on one of these very tugs, H.M.R.T. Samsonia.

This 'Flower Class' Corvette is seen to be 'enjoying' a typical days escort duty in the North Atlantic. More often than not the seas were much rougher than this!

We hit the usual dense fog again as we approached the Grand Banks off Newfoundland. We had hardly entered the fog when we heard a mighty explosion astern, followed by many more. The whole fog bank itself turned a bright red colour. An ammunition ship had been torpedoed. It must, hopefully, have been a mercifully quick end for its crew! The explosions continued for some time, echoing through our engine room. Perhaps by now some of them were depth Charges being dropped by our escorts as they searched for the U-Boat that did this.

The massive power of one Depth Charge, Imagine a pattern of 10!

For us down below it was like being in a tin can with someone beating it on the outside. We hoped they got the U-Boat. As I said earlier, they liked to wait at the edge of the fog banks. This one must have taken his aim just as the ship was about to enter the fog. We sailed on, muttering our thoughtful, silent prayers, for those that had just departed this world and hoping it would not be our turn next! Torpedoing was so instant. One minute you are sailing peacefully along, the next you are hit without any warning. No more ships were hit that night because of the fog, but we were to lose another 5 ships before we reached England.

It was a couple of days before we emerged from the fog. The sudden silence of the ships whistles was blissful, but took a while to get used to again. The convoy manoeuvred as each ship endeavoured to get into her proper position once more.

Escorts were chasing all over the place no doubt 'pinging' with their Asdics looking for the U-Boats. A Catalina Flying boat out from Newfoundland flew around us for as long as it could, keeping the U-Boats down.

We soon reached what is known as the Air Gap. This is the middle section of the North Atlantic where no aircraft could reach us from either side. It usually took 3-4 days for us to cross this gap which was where we were most vulnerable to U-Boat attack.

Sure enough, the attack started one night. I vividly recall the horrifying sight of an Oil Tanker that had kept us company on our starboard side since we left Sydney, being torpedoed. She was probably carrying aviation fuel for the allied forces. One minute she was there, the next she went up with a mighty explosion. A tremendous fireball rose high in the sky illuminating the whole convoy. I watched some of the crew trying to launch a lifeboat among the flames. Others, with their clothes alight, had no alternative other than to jump into the already blazing sea around their ship. It was the most ghastly scene from hell I have ever witnessed in my life. I vowed I would never sail on a tanker if I could help it!

This tanker had plodded along beside us since we left Sydney. She was like an old friend, always there when you came up on deck after finishing your watch below. Now, suddenly, in an instant she was gone and her place was taken by the cargo ship that had been following her.

The escorts did their best to see if they could pick up any survivors but they were too busily engaged trying to locate the U-Boat and protect the rest of us. The last ship in each column was always asked if they would stop and pick up survivors. Very few did. It was at great risk to themselves and their own crews. The value of a few lives at sea in those days was far out valued by the cargo the ship was carrying, and indeed the ship itself which would hopefully be available to make a few more crossings!

The whole convoy is lit up by the horrific explosion of an oil tanker. There were no survivors.

We lost another four ships over the next two nights. Not too bad compared to the losses sustained in some of the other convoys. Each individual ship was an entity unto itself, and the losses to family and friends of a Father or Son, and the valuable cargo of food, or war materials, amounted to a tragedy for our country with each sinking.

We in the old 'Veni' thankfully plodded on. I often wondered whether a U-Boat Commander looking through his periscope and seeing our cargo of timber piled up high on deck, took the decision to look for better looking ships with possibly more valuable cargo to expend his torpedoes on!

As usual, it was a relief when we sighted land once again when approaching the coast of Northern Ireland. The convoy split up into smaller units as ships headed for their various ports to discharge. Some would go round the North of Scotland and into East Coast ports. Others went into Loch Ewe to await yet another convoy to Iceland and then on to the Northern Russian ports of Murmansk and Archangel. We headed down the Irish Sea to Liverpool on this occasion. We docked in Birkenhead where Pete and I managed to get seven days leave while our cargo was being discharged. We travelled down to London together by train.

While I had been away my Mother had given up her flat in Twickenham. Apparently her bosses had decided to reward her 12 years of faithful managerial service by dropping her salary from £3.10.0 per week to £2.00 per week. I suppose business had dropped off a bit due to the war, but surely 30/- a week of my Mothers meagre wage could not have made much difference to them? She could no longer afford the 25/- a week rent plus her train fares to work every day. She had taken a Bed-sit in Earls Court at 10/- a week. This suited her for a while but it meant there was nowhere for me to come home to when on leave so I went to the Y.M.C.A. or some other Service-mens Club. I used to help Mother out with a bit of money whenever I came home on leave.

Pete lived with his parents in Ware near Hertford and had invited me up to stay for a while. After kicking my heels in London, and spending two nights in Earls Court Underground Station with Mother sheltering from the air raids, I decided I might as well go and join him.

What it was like sleeping in a London Underground Station, night after night, during the air raids.

Pete was well pleased to see me and his parents made me very welcome. We occupied our days by going roller skating at a rink in nearby Broxbourne, or taking a skiff out on the river at the same place. Most evenings would find us at a small back street pub in Hertford called "The Dun Cow" The very 'ample' landlady was a great pianist and we used to have some very good sing songs in that pub every night. Her son Charlie was also in the Royal Navy on the cruiser 'Mauritious' and he was an expert accordionist. When he was home on leave the music was even better. We only had a few short days on this occasion but we were to enjoy some very happy times there in the future.

We returned to the 'Veni' in Birkenhead after our weeks leave and found her almost unloaded. Quick turnarounds were essential during the war. We moved over to Garston for bunkers. I went ashore to try and find Mothers brother, my Uncle Gilbert. I had never ever met him but Mother said he had an Estate Agents business there. I thought I might as well introduce myself while in his town. His Estate Agency was not difficult to find. I recall him being a very Victorian type of man. He wore thin rimmed glasses, a bow tie, a shirt with a very stiff butterfly collar, and had a heavy Gold watch chain from one pocket to another across his waistcoat. He greeted me amiably enough but did not appear to show much interest. I felt he was being polite more from a sense of duty than pleasure at seeing his younger sisters son for the first time ever. I think he was the sort of man who was wrapped up in his own little world and daily routine to the extent that, any intrusion threw him! After a little 'polite conversation' I made my excuses to get back to the ship.

Once bunkers were aboard we sailed again in a small convoy to our rendez - vous point off Northern Ireland again. Another Atlantic crossing in store. The usual winter North Atlantic weather accompanied us most of the way. By now I was gradually building a bit of muscle on my arms and body and finding my job just that little bit easier to cope with. There were still many occasions though when I finished my watch too exhausted to even wash, let alone go for some food or to my bunk! On such occasions I would just lie down on a pile of coal in the bunkers and drop off into a dead sleep for eight hours until it was my watch again.

We had the usual U-Boat alarms most nights. The very loud alarm bell was right outside my cabin door. On more than one occasion, when I did sleep in my cabin, I was told of impending attacks the next morning. "Didn't you hear the alarm bell go off?" I would be asked. I was so tired that even that did not waken me.

We lost no ships on this outward bound convoy and eventually, having sailed through the Grand Banks off Newfoundland once again, we arrived in Halifax.

The ships Agent came out to the anchorage and brought some money with him so we could hopefully draw some pay and go ashore. I might mention that we were relatively well paid on Norwegian ships as opposed to the British. Pete and I got £7 per week and paid no income tax as we were British subjects, but living and working on Norwegian 'soil'. This was quite a substantial income in those days. Mind you, we earned every penny of it! After a 3 week crossing therefore we would have £21 available to spend if we wanted it. This was like a fortune among the bright lights of Canada and America! It was more than twice what we would be paid on British ships.

We got ashore that afternoon and headed for the same Diner as before. We felt like regulars already. As we got the liberty boat to take us ashore our minds were already concentrated on those 16 oz. 'T' Bone Steaks with mixed grill, and Apple Pie and Ice Cream to follow!

Tom had decided he had had enough of the 'Veni' and was going home to Glace Bay the following day. Pete and I were sorry to be losing him. We had some great runs ashore together and built up a firm friendship. As we were walking up Barrington St. Tom said we ought to have a souvenir to remember each other by. He had hardly got the words out of his mouth when we passed by a Tattooist Shop. We stopped and looked at each other! A quick decision was made. What better reminder of our travels together than a permanent tattoo? Didn't ALL sailors have tattoo's sooner or later ? The tattooist was a man called Snow. We looked around his small shop at the numerous fascinating examples of his work. I shuddered at most of them. However, I felt I had to go ahead in agreement with the others. I settled for a simple sailing ship with a Red Sunset background and half a dozen gulls flying around. I had it on my left arm and was quite proud of it at the time. It only cost me $1.00. My Mother was quite horrified when she saw it. "How could you be so stupid" she remonstrated. That is on for life.

I must confess to regretting it in later years. The sunset has faded and the sailing ship almost merged into a blob of ink. But, it is one of the things that immature young men do on the spur of the moment!

I remember walking along Barrington St. on my own the next day when I was stopped by a very buxom, brassy blond lady. She asked me "How is your tattoo sailor?" I wondered how she knew about it and asked her as much? It turns out she was Mr. Snow's daughter and had seen us in the shop the previous day. I had a bit of lint and sticking plaster over it until it had healed. Oh. Give it a day or two she said, It'll be O.K. She then proceeded to lift up her skirt, revealing a woman's head wearing a large halo type hat at an angle on each of her thighs. She then rolled up her sleeves to show me that each arm was heavily tattooed. She told me she had a large rose on each breast. I urged her not to show me those in the middle of the street! !Tell you what" she said. "Meet me in the Victoria Hotel at 7 p.m. Bring a bottle of Scotch with you and I'll show you the rest of them" My mind boggled! Being the young 'innocent' that I was, my face went totally red with embarrassment and I almost ran back to my ship scared out of my life. She would have had me for breakfast!

We sailed again the next day, turning south as we left Halifax harbour so we knew we were not going back to Pictou thank goodness! Speculation was rife that we would be going to one of the American ports. Even New York! It was not long before we discovered our destination though. We suddenly took a sharp turn to starboard, and then another shortly afterwards. As we headed up the Bay of Fundy to St. John, New Brunswick.

The Bay of Fundy is noted for its terrific tides. The water rises and lowers by 40 ft. at a time. The highest tides in the world I believe. The 'Veni' had never travelled so fast in her life as when we raced up the Bay on the flood tide! As there were no locks at St. John the trick was to reach the wharf at the top of the tide when the water was slack. This made it a lot easier to get alongside the quay and tie up. As we were light ship the quayside looked a long way down when we tied up at high water. The gangway was almost vertical down to the quayside. However, at low tide, the reverse was the case! You had to look right up at the quay and it was a very stiff climb to get ashore.

These tides necessitated the deck crews keeping permanent watches day and night. They had to slacken or tighten the mooring ropes and wires as the tide rose and fell. Steam also had to be maintained in the boilers to operate the winches for them. Needless to say our nightly sleep was disturbed as the winches were operated!

We spent two weeks in St. John loading a mixed cargo. Crates of Oranges (Most likely grown in Florida) great big roundels of Canadian Cheddar Cheese, and case upon case of dried egg powder. The rest of our capacity was made up with the inevitable timber with the usual deck cargo stacked up to the bridge.

St. John is the Capital of the Province of New Brunswick. I found it to be a very nice town, reminiscent of a typical English County town. The province is noted for its apple orchards and the countryside is very like that of Kent. We enjoyed our stay, but found nothing of particular interest to hold us there, so were pleased when sailing time came once again.

We sailed as the tide started to ebb and 'whizzed' down the Bay again to rendezvous with convoys coming up from the Caribbean and American Ports. Other ships from Halifax, Sydney and Newfoundland also soon joined us making up a huge convoy of some 80 ships.

By this time in the war a new innovation had been implemented. Some suitable merchant ships had been fitted with a catapult going from the front of the foremast out over the bows. This would launch a Hurricane fighter plane that also carried some small bombs. These were known as CAM ships (Catapult Assisted Merchant) If any U-Boats were picked up by Radar, or even were suspected of being in the area, the plane would be launched, weather permitting, to attack it. One could not help feeling sorry for these Pilots though! Once launched the plane could only ditch into the sea on return. They would ditch as near as possible to an escort vessel but still had only a 50-50 chance of surviving the crash landing and then the icy waters of the North Atlantic. Very brave men these!!

CAM ship ss. Empire Tide

The Sea Hurricane and its Pilots, Fl.Lt. D.R.Turley-George(left), and Flying Officer C.Fenwick (right)

U-Boats were abundant in the North Atlantic at this time. 'Wolf Packs' of 50-60 of them would stretch right across the paths of the convoy routes. We could not escape them. Night after night the alarms would sound. Parachute flares would light up the sky as the escorts spotted one on the surface and went in to attack it. The continuous echoes of depth charges being dropped did nothing to allay the fears we held while working down below! A torpedo could come through that 1/8" plating at any minute! For many it did.

A surfaced U-Boat. With a surface speed of 17-18 knots they could easily run rings round a 6-7 knot convoy. That is why it was so important to have air cover to keep them down where a maximum of 7 knots was the best they could do.

We had learned to differentiate between the sounds of torpedo hits and depth charges by now. The third sound that could be distinctly heard down below was that of sinking ships cargoes, boilers and bulkheads breaking free as they went down, and the ship itself breaking up. You could not allow yourself too much time to think about what was going on. The next one might be you! You just lost yourself in your work and tried to keep your mind off it!

We were advised by the Commodore that other convoys ahead and astern of us were being attacked, and to keep a good lookout at all times. To compound these worries we were also informed that a German Pocket Battleship, believed to be the mighty Deutschland, was loose in the North

Atlantic. She could have decimated the convoy on her own from 20 miles away.

*German Pocket Battleship "**Deutschland**" (later renamed Lutzow)*

We had a bad crossing this trip. The escorts had been worked to a frazzle. Their crews must have been absolutely exhausted through lack of sleep and hot meals. Their small ships were continuously awash from the heavy seas. Clothes were permanently soaking wet with no chance to dry them. Mess decks were in a state of chaos. Showers were impossible to take. Life was extremely hard in these Corvettes and Armed Trawlers!

Gunners on watch in an escort ship. Cold, wet and often sea sick. This was no 'Duck shoot!

A helmsman's eye view of where he is steering, the ship fighting his efforts with every wave.

Two troopships, "Cristobal" and "Wakefield", plough ahead at high speed through heavy seas. Virtually immune from U-Boat attack because of their high speed these heavily protected troop convoys escaped the terrible punishment of the slow trade convoys.

The U-Boats were having a 'field day'. We lost 10 ships during the crossing. Whereas every cargo was of immense value to the Nation as a whole, some of the ships carried things like bombers, railway engines and tanks on deck. Every inch of space on every ship was utilised. Thousands of tons, worth millions of pounds, were sent to the bottom of the Atlantic during the War. Not to mention the many fine ships and very courageous men who sailed in them!

We plodded our weary way home and survived once more to discharge our cargo once again in Liverpool. There was always a lot of pilfering went on due to the shortages of food during the war. Our cargo was no exception. The crafty dockers would 'accidentally' drop a sling on deck and crates of oranges or egg powder would break open. As the cases had broken open by 'accident' they felt entitled to take the damaged goods home. A lot of people adopted the 'every man for himself' attitude at that time.

Pete and I managed a few days leave in London and Ware again before we had to return aboard. We often talked about leaving the 'Veni' and looking for a better ship. Certainly not a coal burner! But somehow we seemed to have become attached to her and the rest of the crew. Also the pay was good, so we stayed.

We left England for our third East to West crossing of the North Atlantic in the 'Veni'. It was early December 1942 and we were pretty sure we would spend Christmas at sea. We did.

The crossing was fairly uneventful. The usual severe gales and fog that made life uncomfortable to say the least! We were used to that by now and expected it. I guess I was fortunate that I never suffered from sea sickness. Perhaps I never had time to think about it !

We had a change of track on this voyage. When the convoy split up off Newfoundland, instead of us joining the usual Halifax section, we found ourselves taking the southern route towards American ports. We eventually entered the bay at Boston, Massachusetts, and thought this was our destination. But no! We took a Pilot on board and sailed on down through the Cape Cod Canal, past the famous Martha's Vineyard and on to New York. This was quite an exciting change for us. The lovely trip through the canal was most interesting! Old weatherboard houses dotted the banks. The trees were mostly denuded for the winter but those that still had leaves showed a multitude of different colours.

It was a clear day, but very cold. A hard frost covered everything ashore as we set off. This enhanced the beauty of the scene, the frost glistening brightly as it melted to the winter sun. What a tremendous change from the rigours of the North Atlantic. We saw people waving and shouting to us as we sailed by.

The Cape Cod Canal route was widely used during the war as it was a safe passage from the U-Boats which hung around off the approaches to New York waiting for rich pickings!

A very cold wind had arisen as we approached New York but I was determined not to miss anything. I stood in the warmth of the fiddley top over the boiler room as we sailed past the Statue of Liberty and under Brooklyn Bridge. We were then edged in to one of the many docks by tugs.

We were well favoured by having a superbly placed berth! I think it was Pier No.94! Anyway it was at the bottom of 42nd. St. in the heart of Manhattan. This was the berth also used by the big Cunarders like the Queen Mary. Opposite us was the burnt out hulk of the great French liner Normandie laying its side. Whether she had been sabotaged or not I never did find out, but she probably was.

I think it was New Years Eve 1942/43 when we docked! Anyway it was only a day or two either side of it. American Police and Immigration Officers were very much in evidence. Every crew member was interviewed as to his nationality and background. Then our fingerprints and photographs were taken. We were not allowed ashore until the next day when passes carrying these were issued. Armed Police stood at the bottom of the gangway to make sure we did not try to leave the ship. Following the Normandie disaster, security was extremely tight in New York.

It was very strange to us to see the Police openly wearing revolvers! They were very quick to pull them too if anyone showed signs of giving any trouble!

The fast flowing Hudson river flowed past the dock we were in. It was always very busy day and night. Ships of all sizes and nationalities were continually passing by. The many large ferries kept crossing to and fro'. The continuous blowing of ships and tugs whistles and the traffic noise, coupled with trains rattling by on the overhead railway, made sleep virtually impossible. This City takes a lot of getting used to. New York never sleeps.

Our passes were very carefully inspected every time we went ashore. Once outside the dock gates though, the world was our Oyster! Pete and I soon found a very good Diner and marvelled at the terrific range of food at very cheap prices. Once replete we went to the nearest bar for a beer. Once again, only 10 cents a glass? We couldn't believe it. We were not used to the Ice Cold Beer but, when we found all the Bars had a free lunch counter as well, we were quite prepared to put up with that. These lunch counters provided soup or a wide range of Hors D'ouvres from which you served yourself. What a City. There were 4 dollars to the £ at that time as well!

The first bar we went into was quite busy. We sat upon the bar stools and ordered two beers. The chap sitting next to us looked across. "You guys Limeys?" he asked. "Yep" we replied, trying to sound as though we were prepared to talk back to him in the American way. "Bar tender, charge those beers to my tab. No Limey buys their own beer in this pub while I am here. You guys are doing a great job." Who were we to refuse a free beer? The trouble was that ALL these people wanted to buy us a beer. We had a whale of a night out but drank too much for our own good.

The other problem we found was, the bars stayed open from 9 a.m. to 5 a.m. the next morning. They only closed 4 hours a day for cleaning and restocking the bar. I've known Pete and I go back aboard for an early night about 10 p.m. then, being unable to sleep for the noise all around, we have got up again and gone ashore for another drink. If you can't beat them, join them, as the saying goes!

We remained at this pier for 3-4 days and were able to take the opportunity to explore the 'big apple'. There was much to see. The many Cinemas on 42nd. St. and Times Square, each one specialising in a different type of film so you could choose to see whatever you liked best. Ex World Heavyweight Boxer, Jack Dempsey had his famous bar on Times Square. The great Rockefeller Centre with its tremendous indoor theatre and outdoor ice skating rink. The Woolworth Skyscraper, at one time the tallest building on the world but now dwarfed by many others. We visited Greenwich Village, St. Patricks Cathedral, Wall St., Fifth Ave, Central Park and many more places of interest. We usually travelled on the Metro from one end of Manhattan Island to the other. It only cost a 'nickel'(5 cents) no matter how far you wanted to go.

We found a Merchant Navy Canteen on Fifth Avenue. It was called 'The Music Box Canteen'. It was a wonderful haven where hostesses gave their time voluntarily all day. There was a dance floor and ladies to dance with. There were free refreshments. Free tickets to go anywhere you wanted.

Theatres, Cinemas, Clubs, Museums, you name it and you could get a ticket to go there.

I recall having my first ever dance with a lady here! A wind up gramophone was playing 'Lily of Laguna'. A hostess came over and asked me if I would like to dance? I blushed. I told her I did not know how to. She kept insisting she would show me. After a few clumsy rounds, and a lot of laughter, I began to get the hang of it and enjoy it. I have loved dancing ever since.

We were a bit disappointed when we heard we were moving from our berth so close to town. But move we had to. We cheered up considerably when we learned that we were going over to Hoboken, New Jersey, for a complete refit at the Bethlehem Steel Company's Yard. This was really great news! A lengthy stay in a City like New York was a 'dream come true' in those war torn days. Pete and I were more than pleased we had decided to stay with the 'Veni' for another trip at least!

Apparently the trip before Pete and I joined her the Veni had lost her propeller in rough seas some 20-30 miles east of Newfoundland. She had drifted on her own for 3-4 days before a sea going tug came out from Halifax and found her. Fortunately before a U-Boat did! She was dry docked in Halifax and a new propeller fitted but alignment to her bearings had not been made satisfactorily. I was certainly glad I was not on board her that trip!

It was rumoured that a generator was to be fitted and we would at least have electricity and a refrigerator on board. Wow!

Hoboken was a large Urban Shipyard town. Plenty of Bars and Diners! It was even better in some ways than New York City itself. Every third glass of beer was free! The free lunch counters were also magnificent. How on earth did they do it, and make a profit? I bet they don't do it now!

Our favourite haunt was a large Bar, decorated and furnished in Edwardian style. Even the waiters and waitresses were dressed in Edwardian clothes. Apparently this was an early regular haunt of Frank Sinatra. He sang there quite a lot before he became wider known.

The weather deteriorated very badly soon after our arrival at Hoboken. Heavy snow fell and temperatures soon dropped to as low as -50 deg. Even the fast flowing Hudson River froze over. Ships, including ours, were covered from Mast Head to deck in ice and frozen snow. I had never experienced such cold in my life. They said it was the coldest winter New

York had experienced for over 50 years. Aboard the 'Veni' life was horrendous. The boilers were blown down for cleaning and repairs, so there was no steam. The only heat we had was the iron 'bogey' in the mess room. As everyone was invariably ashore it did not stay alight for long.

Icicles actually hung over my bunk in the cabin. When going ashore I used to wear two pairs of everything, from trousers to coats. I also wore the very necessary ear muffs and carried a hip flask of whisky in my pocket. The accompanying winds were bitter.

Snow ploughs clearing the roads would pile it all up in the gutters. This then created a high wall of solid ice between the sidewalk and the road. You could not see the road as you skidded along the frozen sidewalk, head down against the bitter wind. Life aboard became very miserable indeed.

There was a large fine looking passenger cargo liner lying in the dock next to us. Her name was 'White Clover' and she flew the Neutral Panamanian flag. She had been engaged on Russian convoys and so far survived. The crew were very handsomely paid, with bonuses from both the Russian and American Governments by way of danger money. Two or three of our Norwegian crew had left us to join her. I went aboard for a look around and was amazed at the comfortable quarters enjoyed by all the crew. Even the sailors and engine room ratings had stewards and mess boys to wait on them. Clean sheets and Pillowcases on every bunk. I couldn't believe it. When I was told that even the mess boys had paid off with $4,000 last trip, I got even more interested.

The 'White Clover' was an oil burning ship, which added even more to the attraction! I never gave a thought to the added dangers to be endured on Russian convoys. This was, for me, I thought! I went to see the Chief Engineer and told him I would welcome any opportunity of a job on board. I couldn't believe it when he offered me a greasers job. This was a big promotion in itself. I accepted immediately.

The ship was Chartered by the Americans and I had to go down to the American Seamens Union Offices to sign on. They accepted me but, as I was a British subject and therefore subject to British Wartime Laws, I would first have to get a release from the British Consul, before I could sign on. Up to now I had never sailed on a British ship so thought this would be no problem. How wrong I was. I was told in no uncertain terms that I was subject to the Emergency Rules of Employment currently in force in time of war, and as such I would be obliged to join the Montreal Pool of British Seamen. I was livid and argued my corner, but to no avail.

I had already signed off the 'Veni' so had nowhere to go. The Consul said I would be paid $3 a day subsistence money and my accommodation at the Seamans Mission in Battery Park would be taken care of. I was to report to the Consul every day and advise of my movements until they found me a berth on a British ship.

Meanwhile Pete had also decided he had enough of the 'Veni' especially in this cold weather and without me on board. He had not fancied the 'White Clover' because of her trips to Russia so he too went to the Consul. For some reason, they put him on a train to Halifax straight away from where he got another ship home. We were, of course, very sorry to be parting company, but vowed to get in touch again as soon as we got home.

I decided that, with my very meagre resources, I had about $20 to my name, I would at least luxuriate in the warmth and comfort of a good hotel for one night. I went to the large and very plush Paramount Hotel just off Times Square on 44th. St. This was where Billy Rose had his famous Diamond Horseshoe night club. I was amazed to find that a room with private bath could be had for only $3 a night. I checked in there and then. It was just after lunch time and I remember spending the whole afternoon soaking in a wonderfully hot bath and getting all the coal and grime of the 'Veni' out of my system.

I dare not go into the restaurant for meals with my slender resources. I used to go to a cheap diner nearby. I spent three nights at the Paramount and got some very quizzical looks from the receptionist when I checked out with only $9 to pay!

I took a cab down to the seamans mission with my gear and checked in. It was O.K. but nothing like the Paramount Hotel of course!

By now it was nearing the end of February, 1943. I had been in New York for a little over two months. As entertainment and much food was obtainable free, courtesy of the Music Box Canteen, free lunch counters etc. I had been able to spend most of my money on clothes. They were good and cheap AND of course not rationed like at home. I completely rigged myself out from head to toe with new gear. My wardrobe included a dozen of the much prized ARROW shirts. They were only $1 each and superb quality and cut.

Having now arrived at the Seamans Mission, I decided I would get all my shirts, underwear etc. laundered. It was a twenty four hour service. What a big mistake this was! No sooner had I taken almost everything I owned to the laundry when the Consul found me a ship. She was lying at anchor off Ellis Island. I was to join her there and then. There was no opportunity to recover my laundry. I lost the lot. My protests were ignored. The ship was only waiting for me to join her before she sailed. Someone from the Consulate was waiting with a Taxi to take us to the docks, where a small tender would take me out to the ship. The ss. 'Kingsbury' was her name. I have wondered since whether the whole convoy was held up waiting for little me to join her!!!

CHAPTER THREE

ss. 'KINGSBURY'
(Doomed from the very start)

It was dark, freezing cold and windy as the small boat edged alongside the lowered gangway of the Kingsbury. It was with some difficulty that I managed to leap from the rising and falling boat to the lower platform on the gangway. My luggage was then passed to me. I was feeling pretty low at the thoughts of leaving the safety and bright lights of New York and the comfortable, albeit cold, time I had spent there. I had really got used to the place, The fact that I had lost all my clothes to the laundry did nothing to endear me to joining the 'Kingsbury'. Let alone the opportunity missed aboard the 'White Clover'! However, I suppose the thought of seeing home again was something to look forward to, as was my promotion to Fireman. My pay would be a loss. Half of that I earned on the 'Veni'! About £3.10.0 a week AND I would have to pay tax on it.

The anchorage was full of ships and, no sooner had I got on board than we weighed anchor and sailed out. Much hooting and whistling of ships sirens sounded as we formed up in lines to exit the Hudson river. We formed up into a sizeable convoy as we approached the Nantucket Lightship. I 'fell right into it' when I discovered I was on the 4-8 watch! This meant, my going straight down below and stoking the boilers. I never told anyone I had not done it before! I had, of course, had plenty of opportunity of watching the Norwegians at work, so thought I would have no problem. I found it very hard and heavy work after my nearly 3 months sojourn in New York. The 'Kingsbury' had come across from West Africa where she had loaded a cargo of Bauxite (Aluminium Ore) Soya Beans and hard wood logs. U.K.Convoys from Cape Town and West Africa had been diverted to New York before crossing the Atlantic because the 'Torch' landings in North Africa were sending many ships across from America and the risk involved of convoys crossing each other was too great to take. My poor shipmates had been at anchor for a week in New York without being allowed ashore. Very frustrating when they could see all the bright lights and activity going on around them! They envied me my long stay there.

I finished my watch tired, and exhausted, but nevertheless managed to keep my end, and the steam, up without too much trouble, or apparently, suspension of my inexperience from my colleagues! I staggered aft to our quarters along the cold and heaving deck in a really freshening sea. Within a couple of hours of turning in I was awakened with ship really rolling about and the wind howling something awful. We had been hit by a Hurricane to the south of Cape Hatteras. We were soon in much more bother as a huge wave crashed through the bunker hatch top and washed coal down through to the stokehold. This continually happened until the bilges were clogged up and water soon rose to the dead plates on the furnaces. (Shades of my experience on the 'Veni' the previous year) We soon lost steam, and the convoy, and had to turn back to New York for repairs.

Eventually arriving at our old anchorage off Ellis Island again. The wind was still blowing very hard and ships were dragging their anchors. There were one or two collisions. Ice flows were banging against the ships sides as the wind broke up the ice further up upstream. The deck crew were able to do more permanent repairs to the bunker hatch while a coal barge brought us some better coal than that which the ship had taken on at the island of St. Thomas before first arriving in New York.

Once again we were not allowed ashore during the whole week we lay at anchor waiting for another convoy to be formed. I was hoping to be able to retrieve my clothes from the laundry. It was only my persistent worrying of the Chief Engineer that made him finally approach the Captain and the ships Agent to finally do something about it for me. I suppose they had many more things to worry about than retrieving a Stokers laundry! Anyway, it meant a great deal to me. It had cost me a lot of money, and I was very pleased when it finally arrived back on board again. As it happened, I need not have bothered about it, as will be seen later in this chapter!

As we were not allowed ashore, we were more than pleased when sailing orders came again. The build up of ships in New York was so great, well over a hundred, that it was decided to split us up into three convoys. We would be in the slow one SC122. This was for ships capable of maintaining no more than 7 knots. Two fast Convoys, designated HX 229 and HX 229a, travelling at about 10 knots, would leave at 24 hour intervals after us.

Our convoy contained a total of 64 ships of all shapes, sizes and nationalities. The largest was the Glen Lines 'Glenapp'. She would carry the Convoy Commodore and his signalling staff. The smallest ship was a little Icelandic vessel of only 775 tons carrying a cargo of timber. She eventually fell out of the convoy in another storm and proceeded safely to Iceland on her own. The wide variety of vessels in the Convoy included two Tank landing Ships fully laden with tanks, food and steel. There were nine oil tankers and the rest all freighters carrying a wide assortment of cargo from Meat to Explosives, Wheat to general cargo, Aircraft to Railway Engines and many other items badly needed for the war effort.

A properly equipped rescue ship the ss. 'Zamalek' was also allocated to us. She was a small 1,500 ton one time ferry boat operating in the eastern Mediterranean. She had already made a name for herself by rescuing and saving the lives of many men, under the most difficult, and harrowing of times in the Russian convoys.

There were a few of these small, properly equipped ships now plying the North Atlantic convoy routes. They were all very similar in size and did a magnificent job at great risk to themselves and their crews by dropping behind the convoys and searching for survivors of torpedoed ships.

I am able to give more detailed and accurate information about this convoy thanks to an excellently researched and written book called " Convoy" by Martin Middlebrook.(ISBNO713909277)

Our escorts for the New York to Newfoundland leg of the voyage consisted of 1 Destroyer, 4 Corvettes and 2 Mine Sweepers. From Newfoundland onward we had the following escorts - 1 Destroyer, 1 Frigate, 5 Corvettes and 1 Armed Trawler. Not a lot for such a large convoy and, as it turned out many of them were not with us for a lot of the time for one reason or another.

In the event of a U-Boat attack these few vessels would be very hard pressed to give protection to such a large convoy. In any event, we only had so many escorts available as one has to consider the other two fast moving convoys just behind us! There would be other west bound ones leaving the U.K. and the rest of the world also needed shipping lanes protected! There would also be quite a few escort ships in dock for refit or repair. So, we were hard pressed to give adequate cover to all our North Atlantic convoys! In spite of many losses it is amazing how many ships did get through.

Being a mere Fireman of course, I was not privy to what was really afoot! In the light of what I know now, having read Martin Middlebrooks book, I am extremely glad I did not know!

There were four homeward bound convoys in the North Atlantic at that time and three outward bound ones. That must have totalled something like 500 ships. Add the independent fast ships and the escorts. Probably some 600 ships for the U-Boats to have a go at.

There were apparently four groups of U-Boat ' Wolf Packs' totalling some 50-60 boats in all, spread right across our paths waiting for us. We could not avoid them. It was inevitable that we would have some losses, and occur they did. March 1943 was the worst ever for us in the North Atlantic, the U-Boats had a 'field day'

We sailed through heavy storms once again for the first week of our voyage. There were the inevitable casualties of the storms themselves! Some ships having to leave the convoy and head for Halifax or St. Johns, Newfoundland. It should be remembered that many ships were very old and badly in need of repairs. It did not take much to cripple them!

One of our escorts, the armed Trawler H.M.S. Campobello was very unfortunate too. She sprang some plates underneath her coal bunkers and started to take in water fast. There was nothing could be done to save her. The Flower Class Corvette H.M.S. Godetia was ordered back to assist her and take off her crew. She then fired a few shells to help her on her way down to the depths. To save further time she administered the final Coup de Grace by putting a depth charge under her.

We had been advised that U-Boats were in our area and we were in fact being shadowed. We were pleased therefore to have what we thought were the added protection of the storms around us! News had been passed round by the Commodore that SC 121 ahead of us had been attacked and 'Badly mauled'. The fast convoy HX 229 about 100 miles astern of us had also received heavy losses on 15/16th. March,

I well recall the 17th. March! It was St. Patricks Day, not that I realised that at the time or was even interested in it. It was to be a date I would remember for the rest of my life though! I came off watch at 8 p.m. and found it to be a fine and clear night, albeit there was a fair breeze blowing and the seas were still running a bit high from the previous storms. I stood for a while admiring the convoy and getting a bit of fresh air. All seemed quiet and peaceful as I watched the steady roll of our companion ships plodding their weary way home just like us. I remarked to my shipmate standing by me, "I think it is a bit too rough for the U-Boats to have a go at us again tonight?". I then went below and turned in. I was soon sound asleep.

A shattering explosion woke me up. The ship gave a great shudder. I looked at my watch, it was 5 minutes past midnight. The throbbing of the engine stopped and the ship soon took a list to port. I leapt out of my bunk wearing only the underpants I always slept in. I did not wait to grab anything else other than my blue Kapok life jacket. I dashed up the ladder on the starboard side and ran along the deck to the lifeboat amidships. It was lucky for me that I chose the starboard side! When I looked back aft from the boat deck , I could see a great gaping hole in the deck on the port side. I would have caught my shins on the upturned pieces of jagged steel and taken a dive into the hold if I had run down the port side.

By now chaos seemed to be raging ! The stopped engine meant the boiler safety valves were blowing off the high pressure steam with a tremendous noise. We only had two lifeboats, the port side was launched first as the ship was listing that way. The painter rope holding the boat broke as she hit the water and the boat drifted away with one sailor in it, never to be seen again.

The ship still had way on her as attempts were made to launch the starboard lifeboat. She got smashed against the ships side. We looked around for help. There was none. Three other ships around us had also been torpedoed. All four of us were hit within the space of 10 minutes and all by the same U-Boat, U-338. The sky was brightly lit by Snowflakes (Parachute Flares) Guns seemed to be firing all over the place. Whether a surfaced U-Boat had been seen or not, I do not know.

We were the first ship in the seventh column of the convoy, also the first to be torpedoed so we had no warning at all. We watched ships from behind us frantically altering course to avoid colliding with us. We were sinking fast. If we were not to be sucked down in the vortex as she sank, or blown up by her boilers, we would have to jump over the side. It took an awful lot of courage to make that jump! It was midnight. We were right in the middle of the North Atlantic, in the middle of March. Thirty foot waves. A sinking ship ready to drag you down with her, and little hope of being picked up. But jump we all did.

As I hit the freezing water and went right under it seemed as if I would never reach the surface again. It took an eternity to rise. I was quite surprised when I found myself bobbing on the surface of the water, gasping for breath and being thrown about by the waves. The sea water temperature seemed to be a little warmer than the air, and probably was, albeit it was still bitterly cold.

I suppose I was a pretty fit 18 years of age at the time! My work had put a few muscles on my normally 'skinny' frame. I think the older men must have found it a lot more difficult than me to take that final plunge. Certainly I have often thought about it over the years and said there was no way I could do it now!

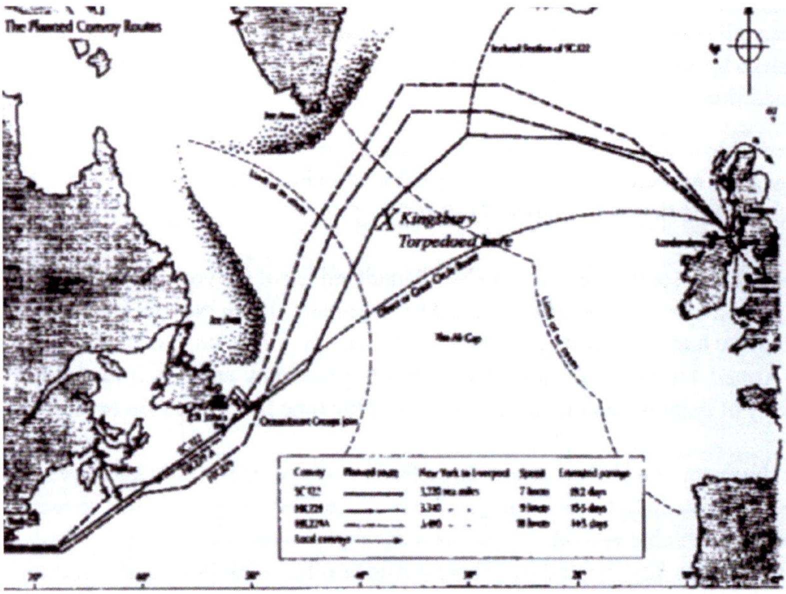

Routes of Convoys SC 122, HX 229 and HX 229a during March 1943

Although there were many ships around me and much light from the flares, I felt very small, frightened and insignificant in the water. I was alone. I knew there was little chance of anyone seeing me and they couldn't do much about it if they did! My main concern was that another ship would run me down!

I must have been floating around in my life jacket for nearly half an hour when, as I crested a wave, I was almost buffeted into an upturned dinghy. Two men were clinging to it for dear life. I thought this was probably my one and only chance and a made a supreme effort to grab hold of the small bilge keel that ran along the bottom of the boat.

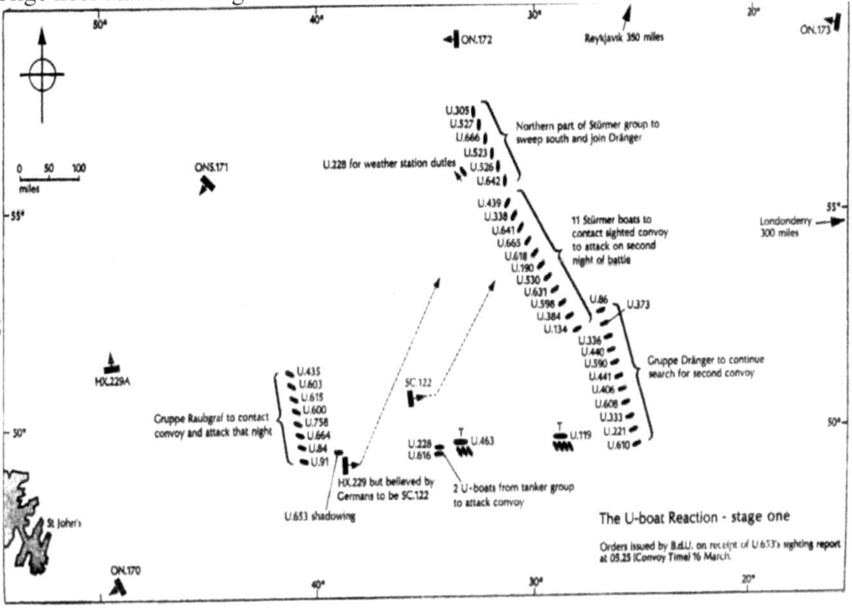

U-Boat deployments in the North Atlantic March 1943

I found it to be our own jolly boat that had broken free as the ship sank. My two companions were our Chief Engineer who was over 70 years old, and a Welsh passenger who was on his way home from West Africa. We all hung on with great difficulty. Our fingers were numb with the cold as we clung to our very slender hand rail.

Our bodies became black and blue as we were continually bashed against the boats side with each wave. We shouted words of encouragement to each other above the noise of the wind and sea. I'm sure it was the shouting to each other and the continual bashing we got, that kept us alive and going! It was very tempting to let go and pass on to heaven sent oblivion than endure much more of this, with very little prospect of being rescued!

There was certainly no chance of anyone seeing us in the dark and, even in daylight it would be a miracle! However, we all managed to cling on somehow and, as the faint light of dawn broke along the eastern skyline some 6 hours after we had leapt into the water, we thought we discerned the silhouette of a ship on the horizon as we crested each wave!

It was not only a ship. It was the Rescue ship ss. 'Zamalek'. There was no mistaking her raked masts, a silhouette we had all come to recognise as she sailed with us. The question was, would she see us? I very much doubted she could. A small upturned dinghy in 20-30 ft. waves, in the grey light of dawn! She appeared to be quite a long way off. I did not detect a lot of hope in my companions faces and confess to feeling pretty forlorn myself! Time dragged on. Was she heading in our direction? It was difficult to tell. Then we thought, she seems to be getting bigger! Yes, she is definitely heading in our direction. Will she see us? We started shouting. A wasted effort at this distance but it gave us a little encouragement and hope. We all knew that if we were not spotted very soon it would be the end of us. We could not hold on much longer and the thought of seeing her disappear over the horizon would have been too much to bear!

It seemed an eternity before she was suddenly alongside us and gave us the shelter of her lee side. She looked huge from where we were but was in fact quite a small ship. I could see dozens of faces looking over the rail at us and shouting words of encouragement. Scrambling nets were hanging over her sides and a couple of sailors climbed down them to try and help us. We had great difficulty in letting go of the dinghy. Our numbed fingers seemed to be moulded to the bilge keel. I finally managed to get one arm free and get it through the wide mesh of the scrambling net. A sailor put a rope round me and, with some willing helpers on deck I managed to get to the top.
My two companions were not so fortunate though. They both slipped under the Zamalek and were never seen again. I felt terrible about this. They had hung on so tenaciously and gone through such an ordeal, only to falter at the point of rescue. I wept for them. I have no doubt that my tender years and fitness from stoking boilers helped to save me. I felt it was almost as if my two companions had both been determined to see ME through our ordeal to the point of rescue, being the young lad that I was!

They certainly kept me going with words of encouragement all night. I am quite sure I would never have been able to hold on if I were on my own!

'Zamalek' (left) heads for a lifeboat of survivors while a tanker plods on.

Floating in crude oil. The horrific scene of torpedoed tanker men.

I was taken down to the sick bay where the Royal Navy Doctor gave me a quick look over. I was told I would be O.K. and, no doubt, compared to the many unfortunates I saw down there, I was. I was then given a large tot of Navy Rum, wrapped in a blanket, and sat down on the steel deck in the corridor. This was to be my 'perch' for another five days before we got into port. 'Zamalek' had picked up 165 survivors and was grossly overloaded. God only knows what would have happened to us if she was torpedoed with all of us on board!

Quite a few of the survivors died before we reached land. We stopped every day to bury them at sea. A very quick ceremony was held while the poor unfortunate lay sewn up in a canvas bag on a board on deck. A Red Ensign covered the body which had already been weighted down with steel bars. The body was slipped from under the flag as the Chaplain read out the prayers.

We lived on mugs of tea or cocoa and great thick wads of Corned Beef sandwiches. Occasionally some soup was made available. I must hand it to the crew of 'Zamalek'! They gave up their bunks to the sick and wounded, and shared the same rations as us while they carried on with their work. It was quite impossible for the ships cooks to cater for so many of us.

I was still in my underpants and bare footed with only the blanket I had been given when I was first rescued to keep me warm. Someone eventually asked me if I would like something to wear? "Not half!" I replied. I was given some odd clothes, possibly from someone who had died.! At least I felt a bit more comfortable. My new 'wardrobe' included an officers jacket with two rings on the sleeve. I perceived a few strange looks when I went on deck wearing this. I looked too young to be wearing such a rank!

The Corvette H.M.S. 'Saxifrage' had been ordered to stay back and give us some protection. She had also picked up quite a few survivors. These were from the Dutch ship ss. 'Alderamin' that had been torpedoed just after us.

Apparently, later on the same night we were torpedoed another 3 ships were sunk, making seven in all from our convoy. These were the ss. 'Granville', a Panamanian registered ship carrying U.S.Military supplies, the ss. 'Clarissa Radcliffe', a British ship carrying Iron Ore. She sank like a stone with heavy loss of life. Finally one of the finest looking ships in the convoy, the Port Lines refrigerated cargo ship ss. 'Port Auckland'. This ship had crossed the Pacific from Auckland, New Zealand unescorted, with a full cargo of frozen lamb, only to be lost a week from home!

We were told there were still many U-Boats about, so we were obviously very fearful of attack. We would have stood little chance of survival in such a small crowded ship. Nevertheless, we carried on searching for more survivors.

On the night of the 19th.March two more were torpedoed from SC122 which was by now a few miles ahead of us. Another British Iron Ore carrier the ss.'Zouave' and the Greek grain carrier ss. 'Carras'. The 'Zouave' sank immediately with heavy loss of life. The 'Carras' remained afloat and we found her the next morning. It was a calm and sunny day, albeit a bit cold. Her cargo of grain had swollen once the sea water had got at it, this prevented her from sinking in spite of the gaping hole in her side. Her Greek crew had apparently panicked and taken to a life boat as soon as she was hit. They could be seen drifting nearby. When we went in to pick them up we saw they were all dressed in their best suits and had suitcases with them. The 'Zamalek's' crew refused to take their suitcases and told them, in no uncertain terms, unless they hurried aboard themselves they would be left behind also. We were a sitting target for any U-Boat that was probably still around!

A boat load of survivors about to be rescued.

The Greek Captain was asked if he would like to return to his ship and try to bring her in as she appeared to be seaworthy? He and his crew all refused. The rest of the survivors on board the 'Zamalek' were then asked if any one would like to make up a scratch crew and try for home? They would get salvage money if successful! There were no takers. I think everyone had had enough by now. This rusty old coal burner took no ones fancy with so many U-Boats around!

H.M.S. Saxifrage fired a few small shells at her but was unable to sink her. While we were all on deck watching these proceedings we suddenly heard the roar of a low flying aircraft. On looking up we saw a British Sunderland Flying Boat diving low and dropping depth charges on the other side of the 'Carras'. When we steamed by we could not believe our eyes. The Sunderland was attacking a surfaced U-Boat. Among the fountain of water sent up by the massive explosions we suddenly saw the bows of the U-Boat rise up in the air and then the boat slowly sank back into the sea. There were no survivors. A tremendous cheer went up from all those on deck. If it had not been for that Sunderland, at the extent of her range, I have no doubt we would have been that U-Boats next victim!

We then steamed full ahead to catch up with the convoy. H.M.S. Saxifrage had a bit more target practice as she tried to sink the 'Carras'.She finally put a couple of depth charges under and broke her back.

A Sunderland Flying Boat gets a direct hit on a U-Boat and sinks her in mid Atlantic.

A second depth charge can be seen in the white circle about to hit the submarine.

Meanwhile we heard of other convoy losses. HX229, the faster convoy about 100 miles behind us, suffered some terrible losses. These were mainly larger and more modern ships than we had in SC 122 and we could ill afford to lose them! Twelve ships carrying desperately needed war supplies were sent to the bottom in two nights. Add them to our own losses and 22 ships were sunk in two nights. This became known as the battle of St. Patricks day.

U-338 triumphantly returning to Brest with Pennants flying showing the tonnage she had sunk, including the s.s. Kingsbury.

Kapitanleuntnant Manfred Kinzel with another trophy! An Australian Air Gunner he rescued after shooting down a Halifax bomber in the Bay of Biscay on his way home to Brest.

Other convoys were also suffering heavy losses in March 1943. The situation was getting desperate.

Fortunately the turning point was just around the corner. Naval expertise with our fast new Frigates which were equipped with the latest radar and Sonar detecting gear, were starting to join the service. Extra air cover in the form of Merchant Ships converted into Aircraft carriers, were sailing with the convoys. These were known as 'Woolworths' carriers.

H.M.S. Avenger, an American built escort carrier, under way with her six Sea Hurricanes ranged on deck. Two Swordfish aircraft were also carried in the hanger.

From April 1943 onward it became the U-Boats turn to start suffering heavy losses, while our own became more minimal.

Martin Middlebrook's "Convoy" has been a tremendous source of information for me. In it he confirms that of our 47 crew and one passenger, we lost only, 3 crew, and the passenger. I had thought we were only 9 saved, but the rest must have been picked up by other ships.

His researches into German Naval Records after the war are very enlightening. He shows that we were torpedoed by Kapitanleutnant Manfred Kinzel in U-338. The same man who torpedoed the s.s. 'King Gruffyd', 'Alderamin', 'Fort Cedar Lake' and us in the space of 10 minutes. I have been fortunate to get a photograph of this U-Boat Captain after all these years. Following his success of the first night of the attack, decoded messages show that Kinzel made repeated attempts to return to the attack but suffered severe depth charging for his efforts. He finally returned to Brest but was able to shoot down a Halifax bomber crewed by Australians in the Bay of Biscay, on his way in.

Following our heavy losses in March, our escort vessels were now more in profusion and their crews had been well trained up. U-Boat sinkings began to outweigh Merchant ship losses. Admiral Karl Doenitz was getting very worried. In September he decided to have a concerted effort in the North Atlantic once again. Convoys ONS18 and ON 202 were only 30 miles apart when news of this attack was decoded by the Admiralty. They ordered the two convoys to merge so both escorts could provide concerted cover. Some ships were lost but most of the U-Boats were driven off by the escorts. Escort groups B2 and C2 were joined by the 9th. Support Group, and by late afternoon the combined convoys of 64 ships were surrounded by a screen of 5 Destroyers, 3 Frigates, 11 Corvettes, one Armed Trawler and one Merchant escort Carrier. Overhead Liberator Aircraft of 120 Squadron kept a constant vigil. When at dusk, the visibility improved, 5 U-Boats regained contact with the convoy, they found the sea covered with ships as far as the eye could see.

Manfred Kinzel, viewing the awesome spectacle from the conning tower of U-338, was momentarily stunned, but recovered quickly and went in to attack while there was still some daylight left. As he approached the convoy on the surface, a Liberator swooped down and began to circle the boat. In a situation like this Doenitz's orders were to remain on the surface, call in other boats in the vicinity, and fight back with the improved Ack-Ack guns they now had. It was hoped that the fire power of several boats would bring down or at least deter the attacking aircraft.

Kinzel signalled the other boats to join him but none complied, leaving U-338 to defend herself. As it turned out, it was not necessary for the attacking aircraft to approach within range of Kinzels guns; the Liberator carried a 600 lb. 'Fido' acoustic torpedo, and U-338 went to the bottom with all hands and her stern blown off.

Manfred Kinzel looks a fair enough man to me in his photo. He was only doing HIS job in the war and I would have reminisced with him over a beer if I had the opportunity to meet up with him in peacetime!

However- getting back to the present situation aboard the 'Zamalek'; the weather turned rough again on the 19th/20th March with intermittent snow showers. This helped to allay our fears somewhat, as we knew we were still being shadowed by U-Boats. Fortunately the weather at both Aldegrove in Northern Ireland and Reykjavik in Iceland was good, so the long range aircraft were able to take off and give us almost continual cover. Quite a few U-Boats were forced to dive, which meant that their slower underwater speed soon lost them our convoy.

About the 21st. march it was considered that the St.Patricks Day battle, as it became known, was now over. Most of the U-Boats had either used up all their torpedoes, were running short of fuel, or, as is more likely, had lost the convoy due to our air cover or damage from depth charges!

It took us 3 days to catch the convoy up. By now the discomforts aboard the overcrowded 'Zamalek' were beginning to become irksome. We were, of course, happy to be alive, but the lack of washing facilities, a proper meal, or sleep in a bunk, were starting to take their toll.

I spoke to one wireless operator who had been torpedoed five times since he last left home, and he was not unique. I commented that I hoped he would not reach his half dozen!

It was decided that, with 'Zamalek's' superior speed of about 15 knots it was now safe enough for her to detach from the convoy and make a bee line for the river Clyde on her own. We had many sick and wounded aboard who needed urgent hospitalisation, and food and water was getting abysmally low. Two days later, on 22nd.March we anchored off Gourock in the Clyde.

At last we knew we were safe. We wondered why we had anchored out though! Why not get us straight ashore? It transpired that survivors were coming into Gourock at the rate of about 1500 per day. When you consider that the average cargo ship carries a crew of about 50, and many of those were lost at sea, it gives you some idea of what our shipping losses were at that time.

The 'Powers that be' did not want it generally known that shipping losses were so heavy. It would be bad for overall morale! Survivors therefore landed after dark.

Eventually, tenders came out to the 'Zamalek' and took us off. We were then put aboard two old Clyde Paddle Steamers that were moored alongside the quay. Orderly queues were then formed down to the main saloon of one of these where tables were arranged in a horseshoe fashion. As we passed round these tables we were interviewed by a variety of people.

We had to give our name, rank and number, ship we were from, home address etc. Temporary Identity Cards were then issued by another person. On to the next where we were given free rail passes home. Another gave us a small amount of subsistence money to get us there.

We were then ushered aboard the next ship where we had a cursory medical examination. It was really a case of "Are you alright?" and, if you had walked aboard unaided, then you must be! Next we were kitted out with Utility clothes. Each man received everything he needed from hat to shoes. It should be realised that we still had not washed, let alone bathed, since we were rescued. Our hair was matted with salt water, in some cases oil as well. Nevertheless, we all had new suits and raincoats.

We were then taken ashore to a train waiting alongside the ship. The train moved off about 2 a.m. and we travelled through the darkness with all blinds drawn against the blackout. About 10 a.m. we arrived at Carlisle. Everyone got off the train. There must have been about 500 terribly tired, dirty looking men, all dressed in the same fawn raincoats, changing platforms for trains to their various destinations.

I waited some time for a London train to come through from Glasgow. When it arrived it was pretty well full up but I managed to find a seat. My fellow travelling companions did not appear to be too happy about the arrival of a dishevelled looking man in new clothes, who no doubt smelt. I felt I had better declare the reason for my apparent smell and appearance. From then on all was well and some people even offered to share their sandwiches etc. with me.

My travelling companions all wanted to hear about my "terrible ordeal". Although I was well aware that " careless talk costs lives " , I felt able to tell them enough of my personal story to keep them interested, without giving away the seriousness of the overall losses we were sustaining at that time. As a mere stoker I was not privy to much that went on anyway!

I must say that I rather tended to bathe in the sympathy I was accorded as I related my tale. As a just turned 18 year old, who had survived a torpedoing and swim in the cold North Atlantic, I thought perhaps I was entitled to indulge myself a little!

We arrived in London about 4 p.m. and I went straight to Mothers place of work off Bond Street. I was still dirty and carrying the clothes I had been given aboard 'Zamalek'. As I had nothing to carry them in I had pulled the sleeves of the jacket inside it, buttoned it up, and carried the rest inside it like a torso. I arrived totally unexpected of course, in this high class ladies hairdressing saloon in Hanover square. A terrific fuss was made of me when they heard my story. The staff had all known me since, as a young school boy I used to go there on Saturday mornings to collect Mother when I was home on holidays from boarding school. I was soon ushered into one of the cubicles where I was able to have a good wash. I was then given a shampoo and hair cut and felt more presentable.

When the salon closed, a few of the staff joined Mother and I for a celebratory drink in Simpsons, along Brook St. Then it was back to Mother's bed-sit in Earls Court where the landlord miraculously found me a spare room for the night for which he did not charge me.

My experience had come as quite a shock to Mother. That her young son (Still only a boy!) should go through such an ordeal at his age was beyond belief! However-she was very fortunate really!

She received a letter the day AFTER I arrived home advising of the sinking of the 'Kingsbury'. She did not even know I was on the ship. She thought I was still on the 'Veni'.

The letter stated that there were SOME survivors but details were not yet known. She would be advised as soon as more details came to hand. The signature at the bottom of the typewritten letter from the Managing Agents, Capper, Alexander & Co. Ltd of St. Mary Axe in the City was in ink. The ink had run as if the person who signed it had been crying at the time. At least Mother was spared the agony of having received the letter before I arrived home and having to wait for a follow up to hear whether I had survived or not!

The next morning I visited the Agents Offices in St. Mary Axe. Once it was known who I was, I was ushered into the Managing Directors office. Tea was ordered and, although I was only a lowly stoker, I was the first survivor they had met and he and some of his staff wanted to hear all about it.

Having told my story I was offered sympathy for my ordeal. As I was then about to be ushered out, I enquired about the REAL purpose of my visit. The pay I was due! Someone was instructed to take care of this I thought I would have about 4 weeks pay since I had joined her in New York! Instead I was handed a measly £5 after stoppages. When I queried this I was told that my pay stopped the minute the ship sank. I was aghast. I had lost all my clothes and personal possessions which was quite a considerable amount. Even a precious bottle of Johnnie Walker whisky had gone to the bottom!

I was told that, if I presented myself to the Merchant navy Pool office in Cable St., Stepney, I could get a claim form for compensation for my losses. I did this and was given a derisory sum of about £20 out of which I had to re-kit myself again. I was then told I was entitled to two weeks survivors leave during which time I would be paid £3.10.0 per week. After that, I should report back to the pool for another ship. I walked away thoroughly disgusted with the whole system and the way the merchant Seamen were being treated by having their pay stopped when their ship sank.

There was little I could do during the day in London. I used to frequent the Merchant Navy Club in Rupert St. off Leicester Square quite a lot. One could always chat with other seamen over a drink or get tickets for a theatre or something.

One day I noticed a tour had been arranged over Watneys Brewery opposite Victoria Station. I thought it might be interesting and joined the party. Most of those going appeared to be Servicemen from overseas but there was one Royal Navy sailor so I tagged up with him. After the tour of the Brewery we were all taken to the sampling room where there must have been over 100 barrels of different kinds of beer. After trying two or three of them the party started to leave. My companion whispered "Hang about a bit, I used to work here before the war. They all know me so we can stay on for a few extra pints." Needless to say we 'stayed on' and enjoyed 'quite a session!'

London was having nightly air raids at the time which were pretty frightening. I began to wish I was back at sea! I would rather face the weather and U-Boats than the uncertainty as to where the next bomb was going to drop.

The morning after the Blitz. The discovery that ALL you held dear had been wiped out overnight as you cowered in the shelters!

I decided to phone Pete in Ware and see if he was home! He was, and more than pleased to hear from me. He asked me to come up. I was hoping for this and lost no time in getting the train to his town.

We were soon busily exchanging our experiences since we last parted company in New York. He had apparently had quite a mundane trip home, while I? Well, you have read my story. Pete seemed almost envious that I had been torpedoed and lived to tell the tale.

He and I were much the same height, weight and age, and of very similar appearance. We were often taken for brothers and used to go along with this. It was easier than explaining we were not. Our standard reply was "How clever of you to guess!".

We enjoyed a very good leave in Ware. The weather was good for April so one day Pete said, "Why don't we go down to Broxbourne and get a skiff out on the river?" "Sounds like a good idea" I replied, so off we went.

We had rowed about half a mile up river, through pure countryside, when we came across some wooden Chalets on the bank. These were week-end or holiday homes. Lying on the lawn outside one of them were two very attractive girls sunning themselves in swim suits. Unlike me, Pete was never too shy to make an approach to the opposite sex! We stopped rowing and Pete shouted across to them, "Do you know if there is a café further on where we can get a cup of tea?" He acted as though we were complete strangers to the area. They looked at each other, rather quizzically I thought! "No, we don't think there is. You are welcome to join us though, we were just thinking of making some". "Sounds great ", we replied. We had better take the boat back though or we will run out of time.

We rowed back to the boathouse as fast as we could then ran back along the river bank to the girls chalet.A cup of tea? They had laid out a complete picnic of sandwiches and home made cakes on the lawn.

They were both trainee nurses from North London and were taking a few days break at the Chalet which was owned by Pamela's father. Pam was to become my girl friend for some considerable time.

It was Saturday and Pete and I had planned to go to the weekly dance held in the Ware Drill hall. The two girls accepted our offer to take them. We were the only sailors in a hall packed with soldiers and had the two best looking girls in the place with us! We seemed to be the envy of all!

Pam was a blonde and I found her extremely attractive. Her friend Brenda was a brunette. We kept them company for two more days before they had to return home, but we arranged to meet up with them again in London.

Pam took me home to meet her family. She had two brothers. The younger one used to drive them all crazy by teaching himself to play the Cornet. He later became an expert and played with some of the well known Big Bands in Britain and America.

Her father had two large wooden sheds in the garden. They were filled with Machine Tools and he and Pam's older brother were busily turning out aircraft parts under sub contract. I soon earned her father's approval by demonstrating my skills on one of his lathes. We all got along famously well and my heart soon became totally lost to Pam. My first real love!

After a couple of weeks, Pete and I were due to report back to the shipping pool. We discussed the situation and decided we would like to try for another Norwegian vessel. We liked the Norwegians very well, and the pay was twice the British pay! We went down to the Consulate in Tavistock Square again and were lucky enough to be offered an immediate berth together as firemen on a coaster called the s.s. Gun. We could not believe our luck. We had to go to Shoreham Nr. Brighton and join her right away.

CHAPTER FOUR

ss. GUN

The "Gun" was a typical coastal vessel of about 800 tons. Engine room and crews quarters were aft. The Bridge, Officers quarters and Galley were amidships. She only had one coal fired boiler and a small reciprocating steam engine. We thought she would be a 'doddle' after what we had experienced on the 'Veni'!

We soon got to know the Norwegian crew and got along very well with them. There was one other Englishman aboard. He was a Royal Navy D.E.M.S. Gunner. His simple job would be to fire the single Oerlikon Anti Aircraft gun we had on board in case of attack by enemy aircraft.

Tom was a Londoner from Hackney. He was more than pleased to have us as shipmates. His job was even more of a 'doddle'. His presence was only really required when we were passing through the Straits of Dover. We never saw any enemy aircraft apart from then, so most of the time Tom was bored stiff.

The ship was fully laden with stone chippings from Newlyn Quarry near Penzance, when we joined her. She was on her way to barking Creek in the River Thames to discharge it. We sailed in convoy. A very sleek Destroyer plus two or three Motor Gun Bots and an armed trawler escorted us. As we sailed through the Straits of Dover we were fearsomely attacked by heavy shell fire from the huge German guns that had been installed on the cliff tops around Calais. These large shells made huge explosions as they (fortunately for us) fell in the sea around us. It was a very frightening experience. You felt sure the next one would get you!

Once out of range of the shelling we were attacked by aircraft. We all carried barrage balloons but these were often shot down. Tremendous flak was put up by all the escorts, and Tom was in his element. I am sure he was praying that he would shoot down an enemy aircraft himself and get a medal! Then we saw our beautiful Spitfires arrive on the scene. Some fascinating Dog Fights took place and we saw two German planes shot down. Two parachutes emerged and the Motor Gun Boats went to rescue the Pilots. We still had our barrage balloon up as we entered the Thames, but a Royal Navy M.F.V. came out from Southend with some W.R.N.S. aboard and they took it off us.

We were discharging our cargo in Barking Creek and then loading 800 tons of bagged cement, so we took advantage of our time in Port to meet up with the girls again in Londons West End.

Our new cargo was destined for Maryport in the Solway Firth in Cumbria. The cement was for a new runway being built at nearby Silloth for the U.S.Air Force.

We sailed up the East Coast with a heavily escorted convoy. No trouble was encountered on this occasion and the next day we entered the Firth of Forth for the night. We needed bunkers so had to go through the Lock System into Methil Docks. We bunkered straight away, but had to spend the night in Methil to await the early morning tide before we could get out again.

Pete and I decided to bank up the fires and go ashore for a drink. We found a pub called "The Star" quite nearby. We were the only customers standing at a very long bar. We heard the sound of bagpipes outside and looked out to see a kilted man either busking, or practising his piping in the street. We invited him in for "A wee dram" whereupon he lost no time in accepting our invitation. It was not long before, with the landlords permission, we had him marching up and down the bar deafening us as he played. The bar quickly filled up and a great night was had by all.

We suddenly realised we had been ashore far too long and hurried back aboard to find the fires in the boiler were out. We were sailing in a couple of hours! We both set to and, with the help of a lot of cotton waste heavily soaked in oil, we got the fires going again and just about managed to get enough steam up to get us out of the locks in time. It was a very close shave though!

We sailed up the east coast of Scotland and round through the Pentland Firth with its very heavy tide rips, then on down through the lovely Western Isles to Maryport.

Maryport was a small and very dismal place in wartime. There was nothing to interest us there and all we could really do was go into a pub and drink. We were glad to find we were discharged of our cargo in two days and we sailed again for Newlyn to collect another load of Stone Chippings for Barking Creek and then round again with another load of cement for this place.

We had a fine trip down to Newlyn in the far west of Cornwall. Little could I have thought that in 50 years time I would be living in Penzance in my retirement! The quarry has long since closed down but Newlyn and its surrounding granite built cottages has changed little.

We lost no time in loading again and set off to join a convoy sailing up the English Channel again. It was the practice at that time to hug the coastline in case of attack by German E-Boats (Fast Motor Torpedo Boats). We in the 'Gun', were invariably at the back of the convoy. We had quite a job steaming her. Lord knows when she last had a boiler clean! The Helmsman would invariably be left on his own as we steamed up Channel in fine and warm weather. I recall a very smart Destroyer H.M.S. 'Matchless', coming back to us on more than one occasion. A very posh Oxford accentuated voice would come over her loud hailer, "'Gun' ahoy! I say old man could you possibly improve your station keeping in the convoy?" The only reply he ever got was a friendly wave from the cook at the Galley door! In the end he told us to cross the Bays so at least we caught up with the convoy on the headlands.

The Norwegian crew on the Gun, like the old Veni, were avid drinkers. There was always a shortage of Whisky during the war and Pubs used to strictly ration it. Our crew seemed to have a 'nose' for it though. Even in a strange port it would never take them more than half an hour to find the Pub that had Whisky for sale. They also liked to take Beer to sea with them. For this purpose they had acquired a large glass carboy of the type used for battery acid. It held about 30 pints of beer and they could be seen struggling back aboard with this at every port we touched.

After twice circumnavigating Britain in the 'Gun', Pete and I decided we would like a spot of leave and then to go back deep sea again. The thought of seeing the girls again was very tempting so, when we were next in Barking Creek we signed off the ship and took two weeks leave. We had a great time in Ware, Hertford and London. By this time Pam was part of my every thought and we spent as much time as we could together. I would have married her straight away but she seemed to keep me at arms length in that direction. It was probably just as well! I had nothing to offer her, and she was busy with her nursing training.

Time came for us to find a ship again. There was nothing available at the Norwegian Consul so we went to the Pool Office in Cable St. We were asked if we were interested in joining T124T ? Wondering what it was, we were pointed in the Direction of a Naval Officer sitting at a nearby desk. Apparently the Royal Navy had quite a few Ocean going Tugs coming into service and were looking to crew them with experienced seamen where possible. They were recruiting Merchant Navy men who would still sign M.N. Articles and get M.N. Rates of pay, but would actually be in the Royal Navy and sail under the White Ensign. Pete did not want to know. I was a little more adventurous though. I also thought, the Germans would never torpedo a tug and if they did, supposing I survived, at least my pay would not stop!

Perhaps this Naval Officer was a good salesman! Whatever, I found myself liking the prospect of a new challenge and decided to join. After all, we had been drifting a bit aimlessly, I thought! I felt a bit of stability would not come amiss. Pete dug his heels in, so did I, thus we parted as good friends.

The home base for the tugs was at Campbeltown at the tip end of the Clyde on the Mull of Kintyre. I was given a travel warrant and told to report there on the following Monday. I had to take a train from Kings Cross to Glasgow. Then another train took me to Wemyss Bay on the Ayrshire coast. From there I took a paddle Steamer to Tarbert, then a bus along a bleak moorland road, over the old ‘Rest and be Thankful’ pass, and on to Campbeltown. It was a long but very enjoyable journey in excellent weather.

So! That is how I came to belong to His Majesty’s Rescue Tug Service. Otherwise to become known as ‘The Campbeltown Navy’.

H.M. RESCUE TUG SERVICE (T124T)

By the end of September 1939 the Rescue Tug Service had been reinstated following its abandonment in 1919. It was realised that a much larger service than heretofore would be required, as the expectation of large shipping losses on the convoy routes needed to be provided for. A serious building programme of Deep Sea Tugs capable of accompanying these convoys around the world was immediately instituted. Initially the manning of these tugs was voluntary, with a nucleus of yachtsmen, fishermen, merchant seamen and about a dozen Masters with either towing or salvage experience. From this nucleus the rest of the crews had to learn the skills required for their new trade. More often than not those skills had to be learned very quickly indeed as a large percentage of them were 'Thrown in at the deep end' especially when new ships started rolling off the slipways and had to be crewed immediately. With some volunteers as young as 15-17 the 'Old Sweats' had their work cut out!

There were a large number of recruits from the Merchant Navy and each man signed the usual M.N. Articles of Engagement at a shipping office when joining, even though he would be wearing Royal Navy uniform and sailing under the White Ensign. He had to abide by Navy Rules and Disciplines.

A new base and barracks was created at the small fishing village of Campbeltown at the southern tip of the Mull of Kintyre in Argyllshire. This was named H.M.S. 'Minona' and the ex Army Drill hall known as the Victoria Hall was to be our barracks.

Campbeltown was ideally situated for the North Atlantic convoy routes. It was to be our operational base until 1945 when the service was transferred to Harwich which had been the ' Home port' for tugs serving the East coast convoys and North Sea.

The value of the service is best illustrated by Admiralty figures. Early in 1943 the Admiralty released figures showing that H.M.Rescue Tugs had brought in 1.3 million tons of merchant shipping which would otherwise have been resting at the bottom of the sea. If warships were added then an estimated 3 million tons had been saved.

By the end of 1943 total Merchant shipping saved had increased to 2.25 million tons and these vessels were therefore able to carry on, valuably assisting the transport of Food, Arms, Oil and men thanks to the gallant work of the tug crews whose skills and seamanship by this time were second to none.

With more war years ahead, the final tonnage of merchant ships saved grew to 3 million tons. This excludes British and Allied Warships saved which numbered 254 vessels by V.J. day. These figures do not reflect those 'So near, so far' cases where vessels were lost while under tow or afterwards. Some of them so tragically near salvation!

In addition to the numbers of vessels and cargoes saved, the number of Merchant and Royal Navy personnel who owe their lives to the Rescue Tug Service grew steadily throughout the war.

There WAS a cost to be paid! No less than 20 Rescue Tugs were sunk, sometimes with the loss of all hands. The Roll of Honour in this book lists their names and how, when and where they were sunk.

It was not until 1991 that some of the 'Campbeltown Navy' living in the Hull area, decided to form an Association of ex Tug men. By 2004 this association had grown to nearly 200 members worldwide. Now known as the Deep Sea Rescue Tugs Association, it is professionally formatted and run, and is open to all Deep Sea Tug men from either the Merchant or Royal Navies.

The Associations Logo and Blazer badge.

There is a 32 page quarterly illustrated newsletter called 'Towrope' of which I am the Editor and Printer, and 3 day Reunions are held every year. We are affiliated with the National Association of Fleet Tug Sailors in America and have an exchange of members who belong to both associations.

Thus, many old shipmates have been able to get together and reminisce in their latter years, and newer members have a Forum whereby they can keep in touch with each other.

ROLL OF HONOUR

H. M. RESCUE TUGS LOST ON ACTIVE SERVICE 1939 - 1945

H. M. RESCUE TUGS

NAPIA	Probably mined off Ramsgate	20.12.39
FAIRPLAY TWO	Wrecked off Yorkshire coast	02.03.40
ST.ABBS	Bombed off Dunkirk	01.06.40
St. FAGAN	Bombed off Dunkirk	01.06.40
TWENTE	Lost . Cause unknown ?	12.06.40
CORINGA	Lost Nth. Atlantic . Cause unknown ?	26.06.40
SAUCY I	Mined , Firth of Forth	04.09.40
SALVAGE KING	Wrecked off Duncansby Head	12.09.40
SEA GEM	Lost . Cause unknown ?	30.10.40
MURIA	Mined off Nth. Foreland	08.11.40
GUARDSMAN	Mined off Nth. Foreland	15.11.40
ENGLISHMAN	Sunk by aircraft	21.01.41
St. CYRUS	Mined off the Humber	22.01.41
PEUPLIER	Sunk off Plymouth	30.04.41
ASSURANCE	Wrecked Loch Foyle N.I.	18.10.41
St. DOMINIC	Lost. Cause unknown. China Sea	08.12.41
INDIRA	Sunk by aircraft. Hong Kong	15.12.41
ALLIANCE	Lost. Cause unknown	19.12.41
DAISY	Foundered Mediterranean	02.01.42
St. BREOK	Sunk by aircraft. Sumatra	14.02.42
St. JUST	Sunk by aircraft. Durian Straits	14.02.42
YIN PING	Sunk by gunfire	15.02.42
WO KWANG	Lost Singapore	Feb. 1942
St. SAMSON	Foundered Red Sea	07.03.42
ADEPT	Wrecked . Hebrides	17.03.42
WEST COCKER	Sunk by aircraft. Malta	09.04.42
WEST DEAN	Sunk by aircraft. Malta	28.04.42
HELLESPONT	Sunk by aircraft. Malta	April 1942
St. OLAVES	Wrecked off Duncansby Head	21.09.42
CAROLINE MOLLER	Torpedoed by E-Boat Nth. Sea	07.10.42
St.ISSEY	Sunk by U-617 off Benghazi N.A.	28.12.42
HORSA	Wrecked East Coast of Iceland	16.03.43
TIEN HSING	Foundered Red Sea	26.10.43
ADHERANT	Foundered Nth. Atlantic	14.01.44
ROODE ZEE	Torpedoed by E-Boat, Dungeness	24.04.44
SESAME	Torpedoed by E-Boat , Normandy	11.06.44
HESPER	Wrecked off Libya	09.02.45
ATHLETE	Mined off Leghorn, Italy	09.02.45
SIR BEVOIS	Sunk in air raid, Plymouth	Unknown ?

" WE WILL REMEMBER THEM !!! "

CHAPTER FIVE

H.M.S. Minona – our Headquarters ship in Campbeltown

His majesty's Rescue Tugs

'Samsonia' – 'Champion' – 'Assiduou's

I was given a rail warrant and told to report to Campbeltown the following Monday. It was September 1943. I made the most of the weekend that was left to me and felt quite excited about the unknown prospects that lay ahead of me!

I caught the Sunday night train from Kings Cross station in London to Glasgow. It was an even longer journey to Glasgow in those days than it is now, 16 hours being quite the norm. The trains were always packed out with service men and all their equipment, and more often than not, one had to stand all the way in the packed corridors of the trains. If it had been raining, every body's clothes and kit would be wet. The windows soon steamed up so you could not see out. The hot sweaty bodies , crammed in so tight, soon had everyone screaming to have windows opened, while others shouted just as loudly to have them shut. Most people smoked, which only added to the discomfort and left one gasping for air. Smoke from the steam engine would infiltrate the carriages becoming particularly obnoxious when the train went through tunnels. As dawn finally broke, I think we all gave thanks that we had survived such a long and horrendous night! As the sun gradually rose in the heavens conversation seemed to become a little more animated when it was realised that we were nearly at our journeys end.

What a relief when we pulled into Glasgow Central station and were able to exercise our legs again! Tired, haggard looking bodies, lugging suitcases, kit bags, hammocks, rifles and what have you, stumbled out on to the platform and joined yet another queue as everyone tried to get a 'Cup of Tea and a Wad' from the Salvation Army kiosk. I found I only had a few minutes to spare before getting my other train to Wemyss Bay so I could not avail myself of the 'luxurious breakfast' on offer!

However, at least it was a nice warm summer day. I found my next train at least had seats available. It was not a long journey, and I think I must have boarded the Clyde Paddle Steamer about 10 a.m.

The warm summer sun was shining from a cloudless blue sky as the old, but very smart looking 'Paddle Steamer' pulled away from the pier. The upper deck was crowded with Civilian and Service personnel and we were well entertained throughout the trip by a Scottish Piper and an Accordian player as we sailed past the magnificent scenery on the banks of the Clyde. Warships and a variety of Cargo and Passenger ships gave an added emphasis to the trip as we criss-crossed the river calling at the various piers and townships serviced by the ferry, towns such as Largs, Dunan, and Rothesay before wending our way round to Tarbert where I was to disembark and catch a bus for the rest of my journey to Campbeltown. All in all, the journey was an adventure in itself, and it was very pleasing to get so much beautiful fresh air on the Clyde after the horrendous nights train journey!

The ferry owners, McBraynes, also owned the bus services in this part of the world and we were soon rattling our way over the bleak, but beautiful moorland hills of Argyllshire. At one stage we had to negotiate the sharp up hill U-turn of the old 'Rest and be Thankful' as it was known. This famous landmark at the top of a mountain pass, offered a magnificent view back down the valley we had just laboriously climbed. There were to be times when, while going on leave by the midnight bus from Campbeltown, we would have to negotiate this phenomenon amid the snow and ice of winter! The road has now been made much safer thank goodness, although I must confess to be a little disappointed when I drove to Campbeltown while on holiday in the summer of 1974 , I was unable to show my wife what the old 'Rest and be Thankful' was really like!

It was late afternoon when I finally arrived at my destination, the sheltered fishing port of Campbeltown nestling quietly in a large Loch.

Campbeltown from the other side of the Loch

Campbeltown harbour - showing our barracks in Victoria hall.

How on earth the Germans managed to find Campbeltown when most of us Sassenachs had never even

The old Victoria Hall after a German bomber found it.

I asked someone where the Tugs Barracks were and was told to go to the bottom of the street, turn left at the Victoria Hotel, and it is next door, opposite the pier.

It wasn't far down the road, there was a 'sentry' outside, complete with rifle and bayonet fixed. I told him who I was and was ushered through the door and told to report to the Regulating Office.

Inside was a large rectangular hall filled with two or three tiered bunk beds. Various doors leading off round the outside had nameplates on them and I soon found the office near the entrance. I was duly checked in and allocated a bunk.

There were probably about 150 men in there at the time. A lot of them hailed from the Hebridean Islands, from such places as Stornoway on the Isle of Lewis. Others likewise from Newfoundland or the fishing ports of the U.K. such as Hull. All expert seamen, who were used to battling the, more often than not, severe weather conditions of the northern hemisphere in small ships. The expertise of men like this was badly needed if the tug service was to get up and running in quick time!

Having dumped my suitcase under my bunk, there was nowhere else to stow your gear,, I decided to go out and explore my surroundings. I found the town to be packed with sailors. H.M.S. 'Nimrod', the shore based Asdic training school was here. There were also a few ships including two submarines tied up alongside the jetty.

I wandered along the jetty to get a closer look at a very fine looking yacht tied up there. This also had a sentry standing at the gangplank and turned out to be our H.Q. ship H.M.S. 'Minona'. She had been requisitioned by the Admiralty for use as an accommodation ship for the Officers of the Tug service while in transit or between postings. Her owners were the Coates family in the suburb of Paisley, Glasgow. Manufactures of the famous Paisley designs on scarves, ties etc. also cotton reels.

Ahead of 'Minona' was the submarine H.M.S. 'Sealion'. I had never seen a submarine close up before. She looked very daunting. I could never have sailed in such a vessel without feeling totally claustrophobic. She was having a rest from active duty and acting as an Asdic training ship for the new recruits in the shore base.

On the opposite side of the jetty I came across a magnificent looking tug. A board along the side of her bridge gave her name as H.M.S. 'Samsonia'.

She was painted all over in naval wartime grey, she had two well raked masts with a mass of radio aerials between them that trailed down to the radio cabin atop the impressive bridge superstructure.

A 3" x 12 pound gun was pointing menacingly ahead from her foredeck while another placed behind her rear mast took care of the stern aspect. Twin Oerlikon heavy duty machine guns either side of the boat deck and twin Lewis machine guns on the wings of the bridge almost led me to believe she was a fighting ship. I suppose she was really! At least she had some form of defensive equipment. Being used to seeing river tugs on the Thames, I had never thought of them in the terms that this one was.

Laid along the towing deck was an 18" Manilla rope with massive eyes spliced into each end. A large Capstan at the after end would handle this. A massive towing winch housed under the boat deck carried a long 6" wire on its drum. Her grey colouring did nothing to detract from her overall beauty. She looked, just what she was, a very good all weather sea boat capable of towing the largest vessel afloat single handed. I was very impressed with the look of her and wondered whether I would be lucky enough to be posted to such a fine ship!

The graceful lines, solidarity of structure and total appearance of efficiency that emanated from 'Samsonia' excited me into feeling that I had done the right thing in joining this service!

I wandered back toward the barracks and thought I would pop in to the Victoria Hotel next door for a 'nightcap' before turning in. I guess I was really looking for someone to talk too as well! I soaked up the atmosphere over a couple of 'half and a half's' which nicely tired me out at the end of a long and very tiring day. I was pleased that I would be sleeping next door for the night and soon returned to *crash out.* I slept like a log, in spite of all the noise of snoring and coming and goings of Lord knows who, throughout the night. Even so, it did not seem long before the raucous shouts of *wakey, wakey, rise and shine, show a Leg, The Suns over the Yardarm* and many more unprintable expletives ensured we all knew the night was over, and, if we wanted a reasonable wash and shave we needed to rush for the ablutions pretty damn quickly!

The local bakery used to make the most delicious hot rolls every morning and someone always went out to collect them for us.

A few of us felt conspicuous in our civilian clothes among all the uniformed navy men but this was soon to be rectified. We were visited by a representative of Messrs. Gardners (or was it Bernards?) the Naval Tailors. We had to buy our own uniforms in the tug service but were given an allowance to do so. I made an allowance of 5/- a week from my pay to them and they clothed me from head to toe. This chap took all our measurements, which were then recorded in their factory, wherever it was, and in future you could always order from them whatever you wanted from wherever in the world you were and it would be sent to you. Provided you were in Credit of course! They must have had a very good system installed. I've no doubt it must be marvellous in this day and age with websites and e-mails! Within 3-4 days we received our uniforms, made to measure. Badges and even medal ribbons if entitled were sewn on for you. They gave us a marvellous service and do to this day.

I wondered how long it would be before I was drafted to a ship! Some new tugs were being built in America under the Lease/Lend Agreement and full crews were be shipped out to collect them. Maybe I would be on one of those trips! But no, it was not to be.

That very afternoon a very quietly spoken Stoker Petty Officer approached me. I believe his name was 'Jock' McKay. He came from Stornoway on the Isle of Lewis and spoke with that soft lilting accent unique to the area.

He asked me to join him in a mug of tea, then started questioning me about my background. He said he had his eye on me and wondered whether I would be interested in joining the 'Samsonia' as a greaser? He was the 'Donkeyman' aboard her and, as there were only three greasers on the ship he liked to find three who might fit in well together. He apparently thought I looked as if I would fit the bill!

I was immediately inwardly excited. The very tug I had been looking at and admiring along the jetty! An immediate promotion from fireman to Leading stoker increased my pay! An elite posting! I then explained to 'Jock' that I knew nothing about Diesel Engines. "Nae bother" he replied. There is nothing to it. We will soon show you the job. "In that case please take me on board" was my immediate answer. We finished our tea and wandered over. We went straight down to the engine room. It was gleaming, more like an ice cream parlour than my previous experience of ships engine rooms. The engines were an Eau de Nil shade of green, the walls etc. were a light shade of yellow, The brass work all shone brightly. I could live here, I thought! I could not believe my luck. "When can I join her?" I asked.

"Right now." He said, we'll go back to the office and get you signed on, and get your gear. We are sailing tomorrow.

I was soon seen to be packing my gear, and was the envy of the few acquaintances I had made during my 3 short days in Campbeltown.

H.M.R.T. 'SAMSONIA'

Pennant No.W23	Engines: Polar Atlas Diesel 2 x 8Cylinder
Length: 205 ft.	BHP 3020
Beam : 40 ft.5"	Bollard Pull : 30 tons
GRT : 1100 tons	Range : 5,000 miles at 12knots.Top 16 knots.

Jock took me back on board and down to the mess deck which we shared with the Seaman/Gunners. It was a pleasant mess deck compared to what I had been used to in very old coal burning cargo boats. Decent looking lockers skirted the ships side. Two tables in the centre had bolted down benches either side of them. Lockers and tables had, like everything else, to be securely bolted down on the 'Samsonia' as I was soon to find out!

I was introduced to my cohorts. One was Andy Fulton from Edinburgh. I think the other was named either Clark or Barnes and came from Hull. I was allocated the 'Graveyard watch' 12-4 a.m. and p.m.

My job when on watch would be to make regular checks on the tunnel shaft bearings and make sure they were not overheating, check cylinder temperatures on the main engines and two generators we had, and ensure all the automatic lubricating systems were kept topped up with oil and working properly. I had to keep an eye on the bilges and ensure the pumps were working efficiently. The only really irksome job I had to do every watch was clean the fuel oil separators. The Diesel oil always had a certain amount of sludge in it and this could clog up the injectors if not separated out. The machines that did this had 34 Stainless Steel conical shaped plates in them stacked one on top of the other. The fuel oil was forced through these plates under pressure leaving the sludge behind where it was trapped, and solidified, on the surface of each plate. One had to sit down on an upturned bucket while scrubbing each plate in another bucket half full of diesel oil. This was a very smelly job and particularly irksome in bad weather when one had a devil of a job to stop sliding all over the steel plated engine room floor. Any spare time was used to polish a bit of brass or wash some paintwork down.

If I had any apprehensions about the job before I joined 'Samsonia', I certainly had none now. How nice it was going to be away from all the coal dust, steam and physically exhausting work of my old ships! The watch below had two us, a commissioned Engineer Officer, in my case the Third Engineer and myself.

The Third Engineer checking round the Cylinder tops on the main engines.

There was a great shortage of ocean going tugs capable of towing crippled ships into port from far out to sea, and many more powerful tugs were desperately needed. A new type of Salvage tug was required. It would have to be seaworthy enough to take all the North Atlantic could throw at her in winter. It would also have to be powerful enough to take hold of a fully laden cargo ship of up to 15,000 tons and tow her at convoy speeds in any weather. A tall order in those days!

The Admiralty gave a British Naval Architect just 48 hours to produce a set of plans for such a vessel. The Scottish shipyard in Leith would be allowed 3 months to build her.

The first of this breed of tugs was named the 'Bustler', and she gave her name to the class of 7 more that would be built during the war. H.M.R.T. 'Bustler' put to sea in late 1941. The second of this class was called 'Growler' and 'Samsonia' became the third. Her first voyage was to Halifax, Nova Scotia in September 1942. Oddly enough I was in that very same convoy on the old s.s. 'Veni'. I had often remarked to my old shipmate Pete about the antics of this tug in the atrocious weather we went through. She was tossed about like a cork and, more often not , totally disappeared in the trough of a wave. I said to Pete "How on earth do those chaps live and work on a ship like that?" Little did I think I would be sailing on that very tug myself in 12 months time!

Getting back to my first boarding, I stowed my gear and sorted my bunk out and then joined my two fellow greasers at the mess table for a mug of tea. They were keen to quiz me as to my previous history and experiences ? I soon told them and, the fact that I had actually survived a torpedoing in the North Atlantic seemed to impress them and my 'status' was raised accordingly. They had seen many ships torpedoed in convoy and knew what it must have been like!

My euphoria of the last few days was to be quickly shattered when we sailed the next day. As we left the shelter of Campbeltown Loch we headed North West to join our designated convoy off the north coast of Ireland. We went straight out into the teeth of a severe storm force 10 gale and I very quickly succumbed to sea sickness for the first time in my life. It was to last a week and be the most horrendous thing I had ever experienced.

The ship was fully battened down against the weather, and tossing about like a cork in a sink with the tap running. The smell of the Diesel fumes and vibration of the engines was a totally different experience from steam. Blue smoke was soon pervading throughout the battened down ship. It could be seen vibrating with the engines. I began to wonder why I had been so stupid to join such a ship as I fervently prayed for a quick death to put me out of my abject misery. There was no turning back. We had a three week crossing to make whatever the weather. Death seemed the only way out!

How on earth the rest of the crew went about their duties with little more than a few cheerful curses I could not fathom out! My pain and discomfort was to last a full week during which time I could not eat. I was encouraged to drink plenty of fluids and try some dry toast to try and stop the painful inflammation in my stomach caused by the continual retching with nothing to bring up .I must say, I never missed a single watch during this time, albeit most of it was spent hanging on to a pipe with my head over the bilges. I somehow staggered around feeling the bearings and looking at temperature gauges to try and take my mind of my predicament. How on earth I cleaned the separators I'll never know, but I did. The Third Engineer was a great help to me during this time, keeping an eye on things himself.

I kept longing to crawl back into my bunk but even there I still felt awful. In fact, just trying to stay in it was a terrible effort in itself!

It was particularly galling for me to be like this when my shipmates knew me to be an experienced sailor! But I am sure they understood that this life was far different than that on a cargo ship!

The wondrous day did eventually come when, after a week of pure misery and pain, I began to feel better. I started to eat again and in a couple more days it was all over. I was never ever seasick again in my life. On reflection in later years, I was glad to have had this experience. It enabled me to know what seasickness was really like and have some sympathy for others. Particularly my wife in later years when we did some holiday cruises. She always suffered poor dear!

After a week of being battened down it was wonderful to be able to go out on deck again and get some fresh air. The ship still had a roll on her, and always would. Even in calm weather there was always a swell running in the North Atlantic. One soon got one's sea legs in tune with her though!

It was good to see the convoy for the first time and look for ships one was familiar with. I noted we had one of the small 'Woolworth' Air Craft Carriers with us so, weather permitting we would have some air cover over the central gap. This was the beginning of the end of the U-Boat menace. They suffered huge losses over the next year and finally had to give up their Wolf Pack tactics.

There were still a lot of U-Boats about though and escorts and planes were kept very busy keeping them covered. We still lost a few ships but nothing like the scale of the previous years. This trip we had a safe crossing and lost no ships.

We left the convoy about 100 miles south of Newfoundland and, together with our personal escort, the armed trawler 'Northern Spray', we headed for our western base in St. Johns. Our 'Personal escort' was meant to give us protection if we had to leave the convoy to take a ship in tow. With the greatest respect to them, I very much doubt whether they could have done much against a determined U-Boat Commander!

St.Johns was a new port of call for me so I was pleased to be off watch and able to go on deck to see the port as we entered. We approached very high vertical cliffs with no sign of an entry until I suddenly espied a narrow gap. We sailed through these narrows to enter a small rectangular shaped harbour leading off to the left. It was abundantly filled with ships, mostly escort vessels. An oil tanker was moored in the middle and we immediately went alongside to top up our bunkers. We never knew whether we might be called out again to the assistance of some unfortunate ship!

St. Johns, Newfoundland, showing the narrow entrance the Germans tried so unsuccessfully to block thus denying the port to Allied escort vessels.

St. Johns was the main escort base for the North Atlantic convoys and prosperity had been brought to the town as a result of the war.

The Rescue Tugs had their own base set up here and for a time it was in charge of a well known personage in the form of Lieutenant Commander, Hawkins. Mr. Hawkins, as he was then known, came to fame when his ship, the Shell Oil Tanker 'San Demetrio' was shelled and badly damaged by the German Pocket Battleship Scharnhorst in the North Atlantic. It was at the time when Captain 'Foggerty' Fegan won his V.C. in the armed merchant Cruiser 'Jervis Bay' when he left the convoy to challenge her thus saving the rest of the convoy while he headed to certain destruction. He lost his ship and his life together with most of his crew in doing so!

The badly damaged, Shell Oil Tanker 'San Demetrio' arriving back in port.

The San Demetrio's crew abandoned ship and drifted for two days in one of their lifeboats. Suddenly, out of the fog, they saw their ship again still afloat. They boarded it and, with the capable assistance of their Chief Engineer, Charles Pollard, managed to get steam up and brought her safely home. An excellent film was made of this epic. Mr. Hawkins later joined the tug service, was promoted to Lieutenant Commander and took over our shore base in St. Johns.

After refuelling we went alongside the quay where shore leave was granted for the evening. Andy Fulton and I went for a quick 'rummage' around the town. After a meal, a drink and a bit of shopping, we went to the large Knights of Columbus services club. I was told this club had been recently rebuilt after a most terrible act of sabotage there. Apparently a regular Saturday nights dance was held which attracted a large number of service men, mostly sailors, and, of course the local girls. It was normal practice to shake some French Chalk powder over the floor to make it more easier for dancing. I was told that someone had substituted this powder for another that ignited upon friction. The whole place went up in flames as soon as dancing began and there was great loss of life. I cannot substantiate this story though.

A typical Saturday nights dance at a service club. Note the two sailors, bottom left, with caps on. S.P.'s making sure any unruly men are dealt with.

It was great to have a run ashore after a very rough crossing that had taken 21 days due to the weather and rerouting to avoid reported U-Boat packs and other convoys. My 'land legs; took a bit of finding after rolling around on the 'Samsonia' for so long!

We sailed again the next day. We had not joined the Navy to idle in port enjoying ourselves. Another 21 days back to Campbeltown. U-Boats had been observed ahead of the convoy, but again, aircraft cover and the good escorts we had with us kept them at bay. We lost no ships again on this trip. The usual fog on the Grand Banks and storms there-after impeded our progress somewhat and made life difficult aboard. It was times like this that made me glad I was down in the warm engine room instead of taking the icy waves on deck. In a headon sea, waves that we called 'milestones', would crash down on the foredeck making a noise like a bomb going off. The stern of the ship would rise right out of the water and, if you happened to be at the bottom of a flight of stairs about to go up when one of these hit you, your feet never touched the stair treads as you were literally thrown up.

We eventually approached the coast of Northern Ireland and had permission to leave the convoy and beetle along at our top speed of 16 knots to Campbeltown. We arrived in the Loch about 2a.m.and tied up to, I think it was No.5 buoy in the middle of the Loch.

I heard the motor lifeboat being lowered and wondered who on earth was in such a hurry to go ashore at this time of the morning! It transpired that everyone was getting their dutiable goods ashore and taking them to Jock McAllisters ' Hole in the Wall' pub.

Some of the Officers aboard H.M.R..T 'Samsonia'
L to R. Bill Stewart (Mate) Cyril? (Electrical Officer) John Cowley (Captain) Bill Sawney (Chief Sparks) John Barr (2nd.Engineer)

There was only one Customs Officer in Campbeltown at the time. I believe his name was McNeill. The Captain used to put all hands down for two pairs of Nylon stockings on the manifest, whether they had any or not. McNeill seemed to be quite happy to have this to put on his report sheet as it was beyond belief that we would come back from Canadian shores with nothing to declare! Nevertheless, it was always safer to get our 'swag' ashore in case a rummage squad decided to swoop down from Glasgow and look us over a little more closely.

We usually managed 7-10 days in Campbeltown after each round trip. This allowed for engine repairs and maintenance, also deck repairs and painting of damaged parts due to the rough weather. So six days leave was granted to half the ships company after each trip. For those like me, living in London, it was hardly worth taking it.

McBraynes bus used to leave Campbeltown at midnight loaded with inebriated, but happy sailors. Most had brought a few more bottles of beer along for the journey. It took seven hours to Glasgow over the old 'Rest and be Thankful' steep downhill bend which it was better not to think about on the icy winter roads! The bus had to make frequent stops on the bleak moorland road so the passengers could get out to relieve themselves. Everyone arrived in Glasgow at 7 a.m. in a state of almost complete torpor, unclean, unshaven and totally dishevelled.

The London train was always packed solid with service men and all their kit. It was a case of standing in the corridor all the way without room to move. The heat, smell and cramp was unbearable, and the journey took 16 hours. It meant I had only 3 days in London before going through it all again to get back.

I spent this first leave with Mother who had a bed-sit in Earls Court. She was still sleeping in the Underground Station because of the nightly air raids and 'doodle bug' flying bombs that were coming over. You had to get down there early to secure a place. Some people slept in what looked like the most uncomfortable positions on the stairs of the escalators. I went down with her the first night but could not stand the noise and overcrowding. I spent the next two nights in her bed-sit but confess the air raids scared me a lot more than the U-Boats! I was glad when my leave came to an end and I could get back to sea again.

We sailed again two days after my return to Campbeltown. By now we were getting into December 1943, about the 5th. I think! Once again, straight out of the Loch into the wintry gales. A lot of messing about off Rathlin Island by the Antrim coast as the escorts bustled about in atrocious weather trying to get the convoy into some sort of order. Every ship had its designated position and in rough seas it took very good seamanship to get there! We were always glad when we got settled down and on our way. We knew we had to get across to Newfoundland so lets get on with it.

There was a lot of speculation as to whether we would get to St. Johns for Christmas! We only had 20 days to do it and the last voyage took 21! After going through the usual storms and fog, we sailed into St. Johns on Christmas Eve. We were to sail back again on Boxing Day. Not much of a Christmas but at least we would be in port!

St.Johns was wearing its winter coat. It was bitterly cold. The town was covered in snow, as were the decks of other ships. Cars were almost impossible to drive here in winter, the more usual form of transport being the horse drawn sleigh. However, a few intrepid locals did manage to drive down to the quayside intent on inviting a couple of sailors into their homes for Christmas dinner. The *Newfies* , as we affectionately called them, were very hospitable and pro British. My mate Andy Fulton and I were pleased to accept an invitation from a family called Windsor. They gave us their address and told us to take a 'Taxi' to their house the next morning.

We got our 'Taxi', a horse drawn sleigh or 'Troika', as we called them. We sat frozen stiff in the back while we were driven what seemed like a considerable distance to the Windsors house. It might have sounded romantic but I can assure you it was a most uncomfortable ride.

All the houses were built of overlapped weather board, like most on the eastern seaboard of Canada. The walls could be seen to be moving on some of the older ones which were infested with termites. We found the Windsors home to be very warm and cosy inside. We were made very welcome. Mrs. Windsor was busy in the kitchen helped by their 16 year old daughter. The smells of good home cooking filled us with anticipation of what was to come. We were offered a cup of coffee, which rather surprised us! We were hoping for something a little stronger to warm us up!

Having exchanged a lot of small talk such as, where we came from, what were things like at home, was life really hard at sea? Mr. Windsor suddenly asked us if we would like to go and see his potting shed at the bottom of the garden? We could not think of anything worse! We had only just got warmed up and he wanted us to go out in the freezing cold again! He kept pressing us, so we thought we had better oblige him. Once in the shed, which was out of sight of the house, he produced a bottle of whisky. He apologised most sincerely that his wife would not allow drink in the house. He was also an abstainer. However- he thought we would be most disappointed if we did not have a drink on Christmas day, hence his subterfuge. After all, he thought, all sailors drink – don't they? We certainly welcomed a couple of tots each and appreciated the risks he was taking with his wife. She must have smelt the whisky on our breath when we returned to the house, and probably wondered why on earth Dad was taking us down to his potting shed. If she suspected anything, she said nothing. Perhaps after we had gone she did!

We enjoyed a wonderful Christmas dinner, albeit without another drink. After dinner it was suggested that we have a sing song round the piano. There were no TV's in those days! I well remember Mrs. Windsor plonking away on the piano, rather like an old school mistress, while their daughter sang songs like "Jenny with the light brown hair". Andy and I joined in as much as possible in deference to our hosts. We kept glancing at each other though and wondering how we could extricate ourselves without appearing to be impolite.

Eventually, not being able to take any more, I looked at my watch and said something like "Good gracious Andy, look at the time. I hope we can get our 'Troika' back in time for the first Dog watch or we will be in trouble!" (In fact we did not work Dog watches in the tug service.) We also said that we were devastated that, as we were sailing again the next day we would like to get in an early nights sleep without the ship rolling about all over the place. We were profuse in our thanks for a wonderful day, and they phoned for our 'Troika' to come and collect us. Once outside, we both commented on our bad luck in finding a 'dry' house for Christmas. Without exception the rest of our shipmates had a much more enjoyable time. However, we were still very grateful to the Windsor's for their hospitality and a great meal.

We got the 'Troika' to drop us off at the Knights of Columbus club where we spent the rest of the evening.

We sailed the next morning. It was a beautiful sunny day with absolutely no wind. The snow sparkled over the town and hills making a wonderful picture

A cargo ship, the s.s. 'Kelmscott' sailed with us, also a Flower Class Corvette as escort. The 'Kelmscott' was owned by the Newspaper Group of that name and was engaged in the wood pulp and Newsprint trade. She had been sabotaged some months earlier and been in dry dock getting repaired ever since.

An iceberg trying to succeed where the Germans failed in closing the entrance to St.Johns. Icebergs float down in the Labrador current from Greenland in early summer.

It sometimes got a 'little chilly' in northern waters! Small ships especially, were very prone to capsizing with the weight of ice on deck and superstructure unless it was regularly chipped away with axes.

We all sailed out through the narrows in line ahead and met a flat calm, glassy looking sea shimmering in the sunlight. About a mile out, I was standing on deck admiring the receding Newfoundland coastline, when I suddenly heard a loud explosion. The 'Kelmscott' was smoking badly and listing to port. A torpedo was the immediate reaction and we were sitting targets. Full speed ahead was rung down to the engine room and we circled the 'Kelmscott', while the Corvette chased around looking for the U-Boat with her Asdics.

It was eventually decided there was no U-Boat and she had probably been sabotaged again in the hope that she would sink in the narrows and block the harbour entrance. If that were so, the perpetrators got their timing wrong.

She did not appear to be sinking so the problem was, what to do with her ? We hung around until later in the afternoon to ensure she was NOT in a sinking condition. Senior authorities came out inspect her. Hurried conferences were held. It was a risky situation! If she did sink while being towed in it would be a disaster! Eventually it was decided that little risk was involved and we towed her back in. She went straight back into the dry dock where she had recently spent so many weeks. There would appear to be saboteurs around somewhere on the island. However, in a book I have recently read, some 55 years later, German U-Boat records show that she was torpedoed by U-845. The report says that it was thought at the time that it had been hit by a mine and convoy JH81 had been diverted. It also confirms that Samsonia had towed her in. We can therefore consider ourselves lucky that we did not get a torpedo also!

Having berthed the 'Kelmscott' we dashed straight out again and took advantage of the calm seas to put on full speed to catch up with our designated convoy.

We had quite a few U-Boat alerts on this trip and the escorts were always kept very active. The air cover we had all the way over was very effective in keeping the U-Boats submerged where they could not use their surface speed to get into attacking positions any more. However, they did mange to sink two ships on the edge of the fog bank. One of those was an ammunition carrier and it went up with a tremendous explosion which turned the whole fog into a bright red. Our thoughts and hearts went out to the poor unfortunates who had just been blown to kingdom come! Hopefully they would not have known anything about it .

The towing deck iced up, off the Newfoundland coast.
Below: Acting as an icebreaker for escorts, off the Newfoundland coast.

The damaged s.s.'Coulmore' abandoned by her crew and found in atrocious seas by H.M.R..T 'Samsoni'a who managed to board her and bring her back into port. The crew were never found.

Apart from the two ships sunk off the Grand Banks, the rest of the trip was uneventful. The usual storms of course made one feel a bit 'uncomfortable'! The winter of 1942/3 was the worst ever recorded for hurricanes in the North Atlantic.

This was the end of my second trip to Newfoundland in the 'Samsonia'. I was not due for leave this trip and in any case would not have taken it after last trips horrendous experience in travelling to London and back.

I was able to enjoy a quiet 10 days in Campbeltown before we sailed again. We had the usual run over to St. Johns, winter storms etc. By now I was a seasoned 'salt' in the tug service and able to withstand all the North Atlantic could throw at us. At this time of the year, Ice flows were an added danger and discomfort as we neared the Newfoundland coast. The noise of great chunks of ice crashing against the ships sides as we slowly made our way through the flows, made you feel you were inside a tin can with someone beating on the outside.

We had the usual run ashore in St. Johns. We did some shopping. Mainly things like Nylon stockings, for wives and sweethearts, chocolates and other items that were on ration, or non-existent at home. The trip was uneventful in both directions. The U-Boats had just about had their day! We had news that we were to go into Govan Dry Dock in Glasgow on our return for a refit and overhaul. This made us want to get home as soon as possible as it would mean 14 days leave for all hands. We spent 6 weeks in Govan during this refit.

I had a nice couple of weeks in London with Pam, when she wasn't on duty as a nurse. However, the flying bombs (Doodle Bugs) were a frightening menace, and now the Germans had started sending over V2 Rocket Bombs which were silent, of tremendous force and even more frightening. I was not sorry to get back to Glasgow and do a bit of exploring around Scotland in my off duty hours.

The dock area itself did not occupy much of my time as it had a bad reputation for fights, knifings, razor slashing, chain swiping and many other ' luxuries' I felt I could manage quite well without! It was a bit nerve racking walking back aboard in the blackout by your self!

The ship was in an awful mess, as they all are when in dock for a refit. Cables, welding hoses, and trash all over the place. We felt our 'home' had been invaded by 'dockyard mateys!'

We were certainly glad when it was all over and we sailed again. We were given a little job to do. We towed the Battleship HMS Malaya down the Clyde to Helensburgh where she was to be laid up.

H.M..S 'MALAYA' 31,000 tons.

Having completed that job we were glad to get back to Campbeltown and the clean fresh air again. We were expecting another run over to St. Johns. It was now about April 1944. We got sailing orders for Plymouth instead. This was a surprise and we wondered what was in the offing !

It made a nice change to turn south as we left Campbeltown Loch. We had a pleasant trip down the Irish sea , around Lands End and in to Plymouth. We were directed to tie up alongside an old French battleship of the Great War, the *'Courbet'* which lay out at anchor. We lay alongside her for two or three days. She only had a skeleton crew of Free French Matelots aboard her. We spent some time exploring her depth with torches. There was no electricity aboard. It was very easy to get lost in the labyrinth of passages and stairways that lay within her vast hull. Later, we were to tow her to Weymouth Bay and drop anchor there.

We lay at anchor off Weymouth for two weeks during which we noticed a considerable build up of shipping of all descriptions. There were many guesses that this was a build up for the invasion of France. What else could it be ? And what part would we play with the '*Courbet*' ?

A lot of the vessels at anchor were American and ashore, we found Weymouth to be crammed with American troops. Some problems arose between the Yanks and the Brits as the local girls all seemed to prefer going out with the more affluent and glamorous Yanks! We also found we could only get 'Scrumpy' Cider in the pubs. The Yanks had drunk the town dry of Beer and Whisky. This 'Scrumpy' was very powerful stuff and left you with one helluva headache if you over indulged!

All ships lying at anchor had barrage balloons attached but no enemy aircraft were seen to come over. The Luftwaffe had its day! As the bay filled up it became very obvious that the invasion was in the offing. You could almost walk across Weymouth Bay on the decks of so many ships.

One day, as we went ashore in our motor lifeboat for liberty, we noticed American troops embarking from the pier into lighters that were taking them out to landing craft in the bay. When they saw we were still going ashore they seemed to get as mad as hell!. They started throwing things at us , but as the only things they had to throw were chocolate bars, we didn't mind at all !

The town appeared to be practically deserted as we landed. Suddenly we found Beer back in the Pubs, even Whisky and Gin in some. I wondered if before the Landlords were keeping it all for the Yanks and charging them higher prices than we could, or would pay!!! Girls were standing around looking for a night out. As far as I could see they were still there as we went back aboard about 11.30 pm. The Brits did not want to know them !

CHAPTER SIX

The Invasion of Normandy

(The greatest invasion the world has ever seen)

Our shore leave was cancelled on June 4th. Activity was increasing around the anchorage. Signal lamps and flags seemed to be in operation all day and the 'Bunting tossers' were kept very busy. Motor launches were running all over the place delivering what appeared to be sealed orders to all ships.

The wind was blowing quite strong and the smaller landing ships were riding hard at anchor. As they were all crammed with troops we thought they must be having a very uncomfortable time, to say the least!

As we now know, the invasion was postponed for a couple of days due to the weather, but was to finally take place on June 6th. Meanwhile, many troops had been on board their ships for up to 5 days. Cramped conditions, field rations for food (not that it made much difference, for a lot of them were sea sick anyway!) sleepless nights and no doubt much apprehension of what they were about to face, did not seem to be a very good recipe for a fighting force about to invade the mainland of Europe! However – that is what many thousands of these unfortunate soldiers had to put up with.

June5th. was the start of it all. The wind had dropped quite a bit, although it was still pretty choppy in Weymouth bay. We were anchored about 3-4 miles out, near to the '*Courbet*' that we were destined to tow across to the Normandy Beachhead.

Soon after dusk, I was standing on deck with a few shipmates, watching all the activity and surmising what the future would hold when we suddenly heard a deep droning noise like a large swarm of bees. It increased in crescendo until suddenly, someone said "My God look at this!" We turned landward and saw wave after wave of Lancaster bombers flying low over the cliff tops. They all had their navigation lights on and were flying wing tip to wing tip in a wide swath as far as the eye could see. It was a magnificent and most awe inspiring spectacle. The flights continued for what seemed hours as they were followed by Dakotas carrying Paratroopers, many of them towing Gliders full of troops and their equipment. Our hearts and Prayers went out to all of them! Our thoughts also went out to the poor French people who would also be on the receiving end of the fighting and bombardment to follow! This was for real, come what may!

At last, the day they have been training for arrives. A Para 'Stick' on their way over and brimming with confidence.

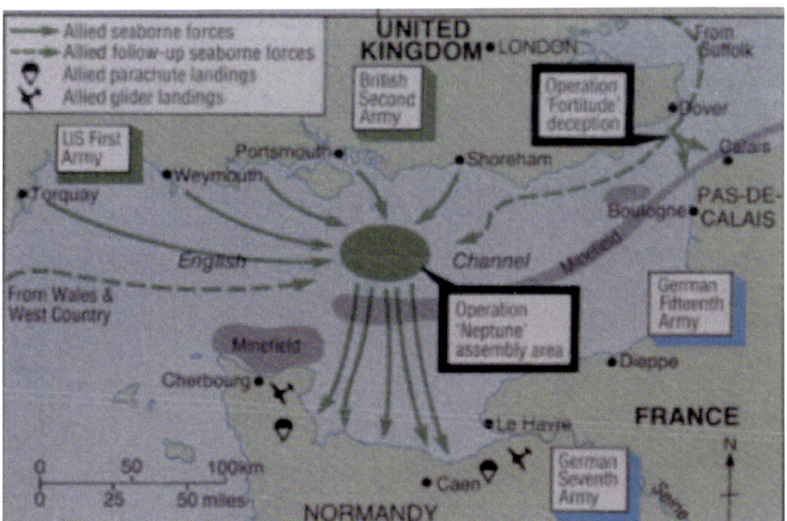

The Channel crossings showing minefields that had to be swept.

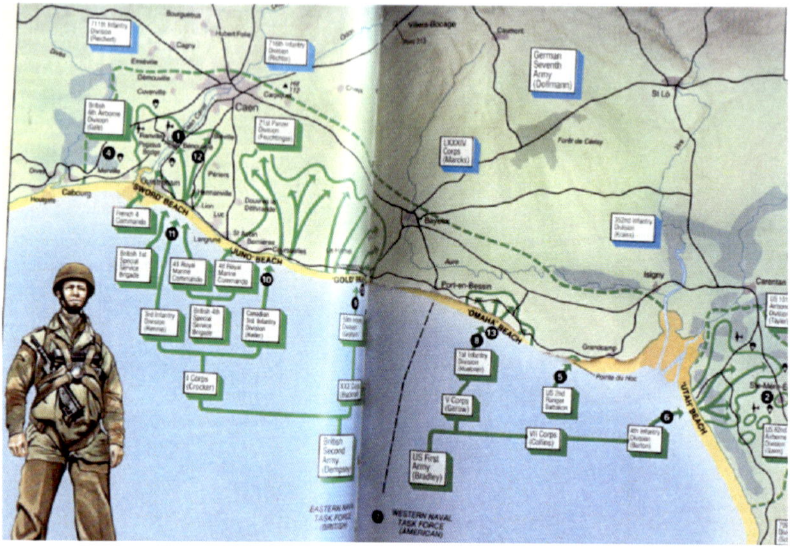

The invasion beach head at Normandy.

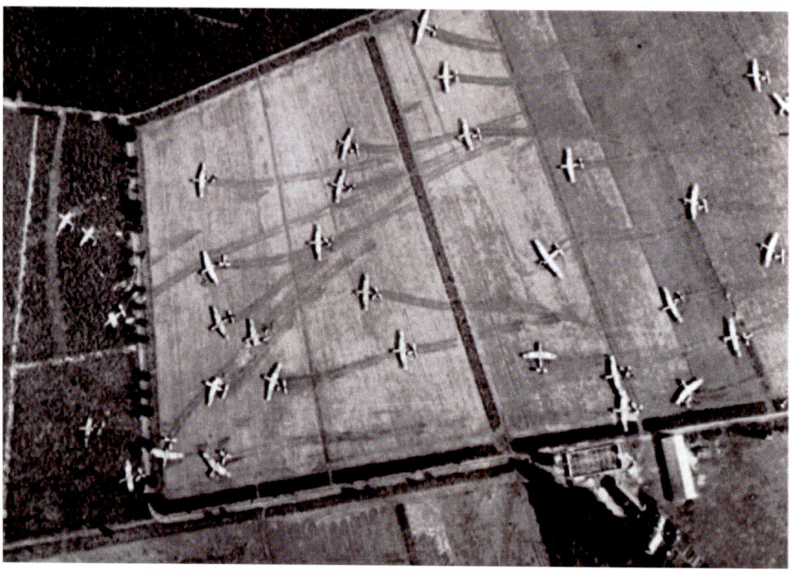

Gliders litter the Normandy landscape after the Airborne landings which preceded the assaults on the five target beaches.

H.M.R.T. 'Samsonia' & 'Growler' towing the old French battleship 'Courbet' over to Ouistreham on D-Day where she was sunk as part of the sea wall.

Planes were still going over when a familiar noise grabbed our attention! It was the clanking of hundreds of anchor chains being raised. The invasion fleet was at last about to start off on its 80 mile run to the beaches of Normandy.

We did not move until dawn on the 6th. We heard the broadcast that a successful landing had taken place and everything was going to plan. Our sister ship H.M.R.T. 'Growler' was to assist us towing the Courbet so we could make the crossing in good time. We shackled up our 6" towing wires and were soon under way, escorted by Destroyers and Frigates. Our 'Skippers' must have had a nerve racking job, towing a yawing battleship among the thousands of ships of all descriptions surrounding us!

Special lanes that had been swept by the Minesweepers restricted our sea room and woe-betide anyone who strayed out of them!

Every hour off watch was spent on deck. No time for sleep with so much to see! From the smallest M.F.V. to the largest battleships all were there doing there own job. Destroyers were continually running back and forth at speed, their distinctive whistles blowing as they warned any straying ships to keep in lane.

Heavily laden troopships, landing craft loaded with tanks and lorries, all had strict timing schedules to kept here were L.C.T.'s loaded with banks of rockets which when fired, provided a devastating and awe inspiring spectacle. I would not like to be on the receiving end of those!

We were probably no more than a third of the way across the Channel when we heard the distant boom of gunfire. As we neared our destination we saw two of our most famous battleships HMS *Nelson* and her sister ship H.M.S. '*Rodney*', firing their 15" broadsides over to the city of Caen some 20 miles away. Rockets ships, Cruisers and Destroyers were adding their contributions to targets a little closer. Our own fighter planes provided air cover and ensured that what was left of the Luftwaffe kept their heads down!

We headed for the Eastern end of the beachhead at Ouistreham, a small holiday town at the entrance to the Caen canal. Another harbour was to be formed here and our job was to line up the '*Courbet*' in such a position as to form the key block ship of the breakwater. We duly did this and charges, already laid in her bilges were blown and she settled down to deck level on the sandy bottom. Her big guns, although inoperable, were swung round to face the shore as a deterrent.

Other tugs had towed old merchant ships over, and some actually own steamed to be blown up in their watery grave to form the rest of the breakwater. They were all known as 'Gooseberries'. In the event I do not think this part of the harbour was ever used, at least not for a while. There was a big German Gun Battery on the cliffs at Merville overlooking this sight. They were proving a bit of a nuisance. Our two 18" gun Monitors "Lord Roberts" and "Erebus", would go in at night, lob a few of their massive shells over, and then withdraw. I think the Germans thought it was the 'Courbet' firing at them and targeted her accordingly! Ever the Para's and Commandos had to go in and silence these guns. A very good book called "The Guns of Merville" has been written about this saga.

Once every one was satisfied we had done our job with the 'Courbet', we were ordered back to Selsey Bill. On the way we saw quite a few other tugs towing what appeared to be large rectangular concrete blocks over. We were soon to find out what these so called ' Phoenix's' were when we arrived off Selsey Bill and found many more anchored there. When put together end to end they formed the famous Mulberry Harbour off Arromanches in Normandy. The authorities had decided that all the main ports of Northern Europe would probably be devastated or demolished by the Germans before we could get there so we had built our own harbour to take with us.

These massive 7,000 ton concrete blocks were hollow inside. A platform across the middle carried an anti aircraft gun and a small crew were put aboard to fire it. Their big square fronts made them difficult to keep steady under tow.

The Marshalling Officer came over to us in a boat and soon had us organised with our first hitch. We were on our way back to Normandy in no time at all. In fact, such was the power of *'Samsonia'* that we had soon caught up with some of the smaller tugs we had seen going over when on our way back. We overtook a few of these and I believe established a record of delivering, positioning and sinking the caisson and getting back to Selsey in 18 hours.

One of the Phoenix blocks being towed from her Tilbury building slip to Normandy

The Marshalling Officer could not believe it when we returned. He thought we must have lost it half way over. We soon hitched up to another one. In fact I think we towed three of these over before being ordered to remain at the Beachhead to provide cover for any ships that might break down or get into trouble.

We lay at anchor between the battleships H.M.S. 'Nelson' and H.M.S. 'Rodney' and the shore. The battle for Caen was still raging about 20 miles inland. We could hear the shore Artillery guns firing and see the flashes at night. The two battleships were also adding their contribution, all of which devastated that City. When the battleships fired their broadsides of 9 x 16" guns each the noise was absolutely deafening. As the shells whistled over our heads they seemed to make an air suction that almost lifted our ship out of the water.

H.M.S. 'Rodney' firing a broadside of 9 x 16" shells.

A long bodied 16" x 2,048 lb. shell being loaded aboard H.M.S. 'Rodney'. These shells caused excessive muzzle wear in the gun barrels, but quickly reduced the German battleship Bismarck to a wreck.

Phoenix's in place at the harbour entrance.

Part of the Mulberry Harbour at Arromanches. Sunken Phoenix's and Blockships can be seen in the bottom of the picture, forming a breakwater. Two of the roadways to shore with Whale Units at the sea end for ships to tie up to and discharge their cargoes.

Some congestion at the Beach Head.

Harbour (T.I.D.) tugs manoeuvring a roadway section into position.

The completed roadway from the shore end.

Hospital ship tied up alongside the Whale Unit with Ambulances taking the wounded aboard.

Some smaller freighters beached and discharged their cargoes into D.U.K.W. Amphibious vehicles.

We started to get a little trouble from German Motor Torpedo Boats (E-Boats) at one stage. They came out from Le Havre and made a few sorties with some success. Even one of our tugs H.M.R.T. *'**Sesame**'* was torpedoed by one, and on the same night the U.S.N. Tug' ***Partridge***' was also torpedoed.

The Germans also used some two man human torpedoes. They sank two or three ships and kept everyone on the alert.

We remained at anchor off Gold Beach for a day or two. There was always plenty going on to keep us interested. The Mulberry Harbour had been a complete success and was pre-fabricated in record time. Large cargo ships as well as Tank Landing ships were discharging their cargoes day and night. The noise of their busy winches could be heard for miles as they discharged their loads into an unending line of lorries that took it all ashore.

On June 12th. a severe northerly gale sprang up from nowhere. Ships started dragging their anchors and colliding all over the place. Waves crashed over the breakwaters. The American sector Western harbour was smashed to smithereens. The British Harbour had a bit of protection from the Calvados Reef and, although damaged was recoverable. Ships inside the harbour were dragging their anchors and in danger of crashing into the roadways and wrecking them. We had to go in and, amongst all the chaos, get a line aboard them and tow them out of the harbour. It was a nightmarish time for our Deck Officers and crew.

The great storm of June 12th 1944.

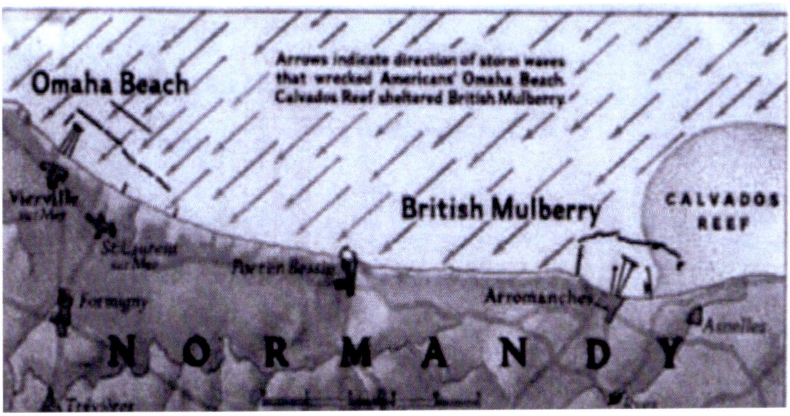

The Calvados Reef which gave enough protection to the British harbour to save it from total wrecking. American Harbour at Omaha was a total wreck.

The trouble was that the meticulous planning of Logistics for the army was in great danger of being disrupted, and to an extent it was. ALL supplies had to be in certain places at certain times on given dates. Any deviation could endanger the whole operation and cause many lives to be lost. That infamous gale could have cost us the war. Fortunately it petered out in a couple of days and, apart from the loss of the American Harbour, damage was minimal.

Apparently the ' Powers that be' thought 'Samsonia' had done a brilliant job under very trying circumstances and , as we had not had any shore leave for over a month signalled us an invitation to an ENSA concert to be held in a large marquee in Bayeux , about 10 miles inland. Half of us went one day and the other half the next. It was a great experience to think that, so soon after the invasion, a concert party could be organised for the troops. How times have changed from the wars of old! The heavy bombardment of Caen was still going on about 20 miles away and we could hear the gunfire during the concert. I cannot remember any of the Artists in the show but it was very enjoyable and a greatly appreciated break.

A day or two later, as we were lying at anchor on a beautiful and warm summers day, someone noticed a lot of flotsam floating past the ship. Closer inspection revealed tins of 50 Players Cigarettes among many other items. A N.A.A.F.I. supply ship had been torpedoed by E-Boats the night before and her cargo spilled out to be washed away by the tide. In no time at all, all those that could swim were over the side and throwing these goods on board, we had a very good haul.

One of the American built Diesel Electric Tugs, H.M.R.T. '*Cheerly'* was also at anchor nearby us and her crew were over the side doing likewise. Oddly enough, some 40 years after the war, I was introduced to a cousin of my wife's who had recently returned from Australia. We were discussing our naval careers when I learnt that he was on the '*Cheerly'* at that time and remembered the incident well.

We spent a few days at Arromanches and, in spite of all that was still going on around us, we had no actual work to do and started to get a bit bored.

One day a problem arose on another tug. She was an old French coal burner called H.M.R.T. 'Champion'. Apparently the stokers were having a bad time with dusty and poor quality coal and dirty boilers. They could not or would not raise steam. Conditions aboard her were very poor. She had two boilers , back to back, and stokehold temperatures in the hot , windless summer were almost unbearable. I forget details of the troubles but gather the stokers were akin to mutiny.

H.M.R.T. Champion

Help was called for and, as an ex coal fired stoker myself I was 'volunteered ' to go aboard and take her back to Portsmouth. The first thing we had to do was bunker from an anchored collier. Another coincidence! One of the colliers crew was a fellow stoker who had been torpedoed with me on the 'Kingsbury' in March 1943. Patrick Murphy by name. Once we finished bunkering we set out for Portsmouth. It was a horrendous trip. It nearly killed me as I sweated buckets to keep up steam with the help of one other. I should have been given a medal for that trip.

I could not wait to get back aboard the *'Samsonia'*, but it was not to be. On arrival at Portsmouth I was transferred to the large four funnel liner '*Empress of Russia'* anchored in the Solent. She was acting as a transit barracks for ships crews that needed replacing. I was glad I was not part of her crew. She had 64 furnaces in her 16 boilers!

I hoped I would get a ship back to the *'Samsonia'* the next day. To my great disappointment I did not. I was instructed to take a train from Portsmouth to Southampton and to report to the South Western Hotel adjoining Southampton Docks Station. This was one of the large edifices built by the old Southern Railway Company for the benefit of passengers in transit during the hey days of the numerous transatlantic liners that sailed almost daily from Southampton. The navy had now taken it over for sailors in transit.

I duly reported to the Regulating Office and was told that I had been drafted to H.M.R.T. 'Assiduous'. The rest of the crew were already here and we would be marching down to the docks to take her over from the Merchant Navy tomorrow morning.

CHAPTER SEVEN

H.M.R.T. 'Assiduous'
(To Far Eastern Hot Spots!)

Having checked in to the South Western Hotel I looked around for the rest of the crew that had been sent down from our base in Campbeltown, Scotland. I found that most were new recruits, and some had never been to sea before. We all have to start somewhere!

I knew what to expect of the 'Assiduous' as she was one of the many Assurance Class of steam tugs that had been built in the river Humber. The original M.M.R.T. 'Assurance' had gone ashore on the rocks in Loch Foyle and was still lying there as a total wreck. I had a look at her as we passed by on Samsonia on a trip down to Londonderry a few months before.

This class of Ocean going tug had a reciprocating steam engine. The single boiler was oil fired (thank goodness) They were slightly smaller than the Samsonia and did not have such graceful lines. However, they were workmanlike enough and had a powerful appearance.

As much as I regretted leaving the 'Samsonia', it had its compensations! The noise, vibrations and smell of diesel oil on 'Samsonia' was not very pleasant to live with, and I welcomed a return to steam, especially as no more coal would be involved.

The next morning we were instructed to bring all our kit down to the front of the Hotel where it was loaded on to a Naval lorry. We were then lined up on the forecourt and marched down to the docks where we found the 'Assiduous' alongside the quay. The first thing that caught my eye was the Red Ensign flying from her mast. She had been operated by Watkins Tugs Ltd of London up to now and the Admiralty was about to take her over.

We were lined up on the quay side when the ships Officers arrived. The Chief Engineer called the Stoker Petty Officer over to him, and they seemed to be having quite a confab while looking over in our direction. Eventually the Stoker P.O. and a new stoker recruit, young Charlie Brown from Newcastle over. I had joined as a Greaser with the rank of Leading Stoker. We went down below to take over the Engine room and boiler. The boiler had steam up. The Merchant Navy stoker showed us what was what. I had never operated an oil fired boiler before. I think the P.O. Had. After about half an hours instruction Charlie said he was quite confident he knew what to do so the P.O. and I went up on deck where by now the crew were all lined up for the Commissioning ceremony. Even tugs had to have this if they flew the White Ensign!

The local four ring Captain in Charge came aboard accompanied by his Aide de Camp. A Naval Chaplain in full robes was in attendance and the skeleton M.N. crew were also lined up on deck opposite us. A short service was held. Then, following a speech from the Captain, the Red Ensign was lowered and the White Ensign was raised to the sound of a Royal marine Bugler playing Reveille. At this point a sudden cloud of dense black smoke emanated from the funnel. We then saw the same coming out of the boiler room ventilators and engine room skylights. A downdraft pushed it down to the after deck where we were all lined up in our best suits with white topped caps. Oily soot covered everyone. The P.O. and I automatically broke ranks and slid down the engine room ladder followed by a couple of Engineering Officers. We found our way through the choking smoke to the boiler room and turned the oil to the furnaces off. As the smoke cleared we found Charlie Brown lying down on the plates looking like one of the Black & White Minstrels. We got him up on deck, coughing his heart out. Everyone was covered in oily soot and the 'hierarchy' did not look too happy about it to say the least!

Brown soon recovered and when questioned as to what happened said "Well the steam pressure was dropping a bit so I thought I had better give her a bit more oil" . He had turned up the oil delivery without compensating with more draft from the fan. This was a great start to the new commission and Charlie was never allowed to forget it!

For some reason we spent about two weeks in Southampton doing absolutely nothing other than cleaning and painting ship and familiarising ourselves with everything in the engine room. We soon found a big problem. She was infested with cockroaches! They were everywhere, dropping into your food or soup, swarming over the deck heads to the extent they were a moving mass. I even found them to be the cause of a blown fuse. They had got into the plug and shorted it across the terminal, what a horrible mess that was when I took the plug cover off.

I had soon chummed up with another greaser, Geordie Moffatt from Newcastle. We used to go ashore every night doing a Pub crawl playing darts. We always seemed to win so, as the loser pays for the drinks we had some inexpensive nights ashore. We had another 'Nice little earner' going for us. Every day an American Liberty ship used to dock astern of us . There were two or three of them on a regular supply run to Normandy. The Yanks loved our Navy Rum and were prepared to pay £5 a bottle for it. Geordie and I were on 'One and One' (One part Rum to one part water) We bottled our Tot every day and filled the bottle with cold tea. The Yanks tasted it and loved it. We made £5 a day. That was a lot of money to us in those days. If we gave them a sample of one and one they would swear we had doctored it and would not buy it. So much for the American taste for liquor!

We eventually received orders to sail round to Portsmouth Naval Dockyard. We were going to have a complete refit and boiler clean, and the ship would be fumigated against the cockroaches. As soon as we arrived we were given 14 days leave. I went up to Liverpool and spent a few days with Mother who was now working as a live in Bookkeeper/Receptionist at the prestigious Adelphi Hotel. The Management were kind enough to let me have a room 'gratis' and I enjoyed the luxury for a few days.

I decided there was no point in me hanging around Liverpool any longer as Mother was working during the day, and I was keen to get back to London and spend my time with Pamela, so off I went. I had another very enjoyable stay with her family in Finchley. Pete was away so I could not see him.

On returning from this leave, I was immediately sent away for another 7 days as the ship was nowhere near ready yet. So I went back to Pam's for another week.

An embarrassing event occurred the day I was to return to my ship. I was walking round Leicester Square in the afternoon when I was stopped by a

Naval Patrol and asked for my pass. I was due back aboard at midnight as usual and was killing time waiting for an evening train. However- The Mate, who had made my pass out had put 12 Midday on it instead of midnight. I had not noticed this. Passes always expired at midnight. The Patrol would not listen to my explanation and marched me down to their office in Whitehall. I felt like a criminal deserter. I was held there for a couple of hours while enquiries were made. They then took me to Waterloo Station and put me on a non stop train to Portsmouth. The Mate apologised for his mistake and sent me straight back on yet another 7 days leave.

I must confess to getting a bit bored with all this leave. Money was very tight. Pam was working at the hospital all day and, although it was a joy to see her, I was really looking forward to getting back to sea again.

On returning from this third leave we were instructed to rig ourselves out with tropical gear from Gardner's. At least now we knew we were going to the Mediterranean. Then we were loaned a 30cwt truck and spent about three days driving around Portsmouth Dockyard drawing all sorts of stores from different warehouses.

Food, Paint, oil, ropes, wires, shackles, grease, sacks of sponges for the engine room filters, ammunition for our 3" Gun and two Lewis guns. You name it. We got it!

Having finished this quite enjoyable chore we were ordered to go round again and double all stores. Where on earth were we going to?

By now the Dockyard Matey's had finished aboard. The ship had been cleaned up. The fumigation had been only partially successful and the cockroaches had soon multiplied and were back in force again. They were an absolute pest.

We finally sailed about the beginning of November 1944. We headed down channel and then made course for Gibraltar. It was strange to be sailing alone after our war years always in convoy. But by now the U-Boat menace had finished. The French U-Boat bases had been captured and the air fields no longer existed.

We crossed the bay of Biscay in fine but windy weather. Most of the crew when off watch sat huddled round the warmth of the funnel on the boat deck from where they could make easy runs to the side to be sea sick. I must confess to being a bit of a rotter one day. We had roast pork for lunch. Those being sick could not face it. I took a large piece of fat up on deck and ate it in front of them. They all dived for the side. However- like me on my first trip on the 'Samsonia' , they all eventually got over it.

As we sailed down past the coast of Portugal we passed through literally hundreds of fishing boats, the skipper stopped alongside a couple of them and we haggled for some fresh fish. This made a very enjoyable change to our diet and the Captain's esteem got a few more 'brownie points' for his actions!

At night it was a marvellous sight to see the lights of Lisbon ashore and the twinkling lights of many fishing boats at sea. It was a bit hazardous sailing through them though.

Eventually the Rock of Gibraltar was sighted. Most of us had never seen it before so, apart from the engine room crew on watch, most of us were on deck admiring the spectacle of the rock in the brilliant sunshine.

We were soon tied up alongside the quay and hoped we would be able to draw some pay and get a run ashore. Mid afternoon we were paid and shore leave was granted to half the ships company. Geordie Moffatt and I went ashore together in white duck uniforms and were very self conscious of their newness. We got no further than the main street with its shops, bars and cafes.

There was little point in shopping as we were not homeward bound. A good meal was as always, the first 'port of call'. The bars were fascinating as most were playing Spanish Music and had Flamenco Dancers clacking away with their Castanets. I could sit over a cool beer and watch them for hours. We got another run ashore the next day but did not have time to explore the Rock. There were the famous Barbary Apes at the top, or one could go for a swim off the small beach. We were quite content to sit watching our Flamenco Dancers!

We sailed again the next day for Malta. We looked forward to a good trip in calm warm sunshine. How wrong we were! A huge gale sprung up. The 'Med' can be as rough as anywhere when it wants to. We had two days of severe gales before it abated and then, all turned out as expected. Calm seas and a blue sky.

On arrival at Malta we dropped anchor in the main harbour at Valetta the Capital. I thought the place looked very barren. Not much greenery to be seen. The sun shimmered off the solid looking sandstone buildings. Church towers or domes seemed to be much in evidence. The harbour was full of many types of ships from naval to merchant. Those tied up were moored in the strange Mediterranean way, stern to the quay. I suppose they got more ships alongside this way. They loaded or unloaded their cargoes into barges, using their own derricks or cranes.

As it used to be! Two rescue tugs come under enemy aircraft attack while towing a damaged oil tanker. The Tanker catches fire.
(Picture from an oil painting by J.Marshall)

We got shore leave that evening and used our own motor lifeboat to get there. I was not very impressed with the place. We wandered round the City. Had the usual meal and a few drinks, then back aboard. I suppose it was a bit much to expect any high life after all the terrible years of suffering and bombing they had endured. We were not sorry when we sailed a couple of days later.

We had a short run up to the Italian naval Base at Taranto, which is right inside the instep of the foot of Italy. Why we went there I don't really know? We went through the swing bridge at the entrance to the harbour made famous by the Swordfish Pilots who flew under it when they torpedoed the Italian fleet in the harbour. We saw some of the sunken ships lying there, also some of the magnificent looking cruisers and battleships which never lived up to their prowess against the Royal Navy.

We went ashore that evening. We had no Italian Lira but we took cigarettes with us which was much better than currency. There was nothing worth buying in the shops, but the place seemed to be full of Guitars. Many of the crew bought one and drove the rest of us crazy thereafter trying to learn to play the darn things. We bunkered here and sailed again the next day. Our course took us down the North African coast again, which we picked up at the eastern end of the Gulf of Sirte in Libya. A little way along the coast to the east of here we went close in to shore and stopped. The objective of our trip had been to locate the wreck of the Rescue Tug *'Hesperia'*. She was a sister tug to my old ship the '*Samsonia'* and the only one of that '*Bustler'* Class to sail under the Red Ensign. She had been towing a large floating dry dock along the coast when a Northerly gale hit them. The Dry Dock acted like a sail in the strong wind and the tug had been unable to hold her off shore. She did not have enough sea room to manoeuvre and the wind finally blew the dock ashore and the tug with it. What happened to the Dry Dock I never found out. The '*Hesperia'* was bow on to a rocky shore and lying at an angle about 100 miles east of Benghazi. There was nothing but desert for many miles around. We anchored and lowered our motor lifeboat. The Captain, Mate, Chief Engineer and Stoker P.O. got into the boat to cross to her. I was invited to join them at the last minute in view of my having sailed in her sister ship and being familiar with her lay out.

It was sickening to go on board and find the engine room completely flooded with oil floating on top of the water. Oily water also invaded the accommodation. There was nothing left aboard to salvage and the ship had obviously been badly holed. It was decided there was nothing we could do and we left. Just as well we did! As we motored back to the '*Assiduous'* we heard a sort of grinding noise and watched the '*Hesperia'* slide off the rocks into deeper water. I was certainly glad she did not do that while we were inside her!

We weighed anchor and continued on our way east. Our next destination was Haifa in Palestine (now Israel) from here we at last found work to do. We were to tow a large floating Dry Dock (A.F.D. 30) through the Suez Canal and down the Red Sea to Aden. This dock had been sunk in Haifa by the Italians early in the war. It had now been raised and repaired and was badly needed in Aden.

We spent a few days in Haifa and took runs ashore to the main town of Tel Aviv. We did not have time to go visiting any of the Holy places like Jerusalem. The main thing I remember about the place was seeing huge tip up trucks loaded with large Jaffa Oranges and Grapefruits coming down to the quay and loading them in bulk into small ships. Where they were going or what would be done with them I have no idea. We all bought them at 3/- per hundred. The ship was pervaded with their smell.

We were soon ready to sail again and we waited outside the harbour while local tugs brought the dock out to us. We were soon hitched up and headed for Port Said at the entrance to the Suez Canal.

This was the first time I began to appreciate what was going to be a most uncomfortable problem on the 'Assiduous'! On our way to Port Said the weather was very hot, no wind, and a flat calm sea. There were two ventilators to the boiler room but none in the engine room. We were only making about 3 knots with the dock in tow and the ventilators could catch no wind. The temperature down below became unbearable, around 130 deg. F. Our accommodation was the same. The boiler virtually took over the centre of the ship and the heat transferred itself throughout. God knows what it was going to be like when we got even further east down to Aden and beyond. This ship had definitely not been designed for tropical waters.

We anchored off Port Said and two of the Canal Company's large twin funnelled tugs came out and took the dock off us to park it. They towed it to an anchorage out of the way of the busy shipping lanes. We went in and tied up alongside Admiralty House on the town side of the harbour.

A first visit to Egypt is always interesting to say the least! It soon becomes a bit irksome though. As soon as we walked outside the dock gates we were accosted by hoards of Arabs trying to sell us everything under the sun. It did not matter that you already had a wrist watch. They had much better and cheaper ones. All kinds of leather goods were thrust at you. Shoe shine boys continually pestered. If you refused they would quickly bend down and smear a white paste over your shoes. You then grabbed them by the scruff of the neck and made them clean them again. When you refused to pay them, an angry mob of his cohorts would quickly surround you with cudgels knives etc. You paid!!!

The cafes and bars of Port Said were quite unique. As soon as you entered you were pestered. "You want steak, eggs and chips effendi? Very good, very cheap." The steak was always goat meat and sometimes Camel. The eggs were bantam eggs and served by the half dozen. The accompanying beer, brewed locally, tasted awful. While eating your meal you were still continually being pestered by salesmen and the Ghillie, ghillie man. These men were very clever conjurers. They would produce eggs, baby chickens, money and all sorts of things out of thin air. They accompanied each trick by quickly chanting the words ghillie, ghillie, ghillie. over and again hence their title of the Ghillie men. They always wanted money of course and, whereas it was fascinating to see them once, to be continually pestered became a pain in the neck!

We soon got fed up with running the gauntlet of all these characters ashore and found much more to interest us in watching the large convoys of interesting ships passing by as they entered or left the canal.

The Canal system was such that all ships heading south went through on one day and north the other. It was mandatory for all ships to have a Canal Company Pilot on board, and each pilot had his own crew of about half a dozen Egyptians who would handle all ropes when necessary and also take the helm right through. Each ship was fitted with a huge searchlight on its bows for night time travel.

The canal was so busy with Naval, Merchant, Troop and landing ships going through on their way to the far east and Australia that we were held in Port Said for about two weeks waiting our chance to pass through. They had to virtually close the canal to let us through.

When we finally got going, one of the Canal Company tugs towed the dock through while we tied up behind it and acted as a rudder to steer it. There was insufficient width in the canal to allow the dock to yaw from side to side, and the cross winds that blew across the desert could be a problem.

Some half way through the canal, are what is known as the Bitter Lakes. On the shore of the larger of the two lakes was a town called Ismailia. Both the dock and us were anchored here for about three weeks before they would let us continue our journey. Too much shipping was being held up at either end while we were going through.
The Pilots crew stayed aboard with us. They slept on the open deck. As usual they had brought all their wares with them to sell to us in an attempt to supplement their income. These were spread out all over the engine room skylights every day. If we wanted to go ashore it was their boat tied up alongside that took us. We got very incensed when they charged us about 1 Piastre each to take us ashore and then wanted 5 to bring us back. They were complete rogues.

One or two of the crew thought they would get their own back by pinching some of their wares on the skylights. They soon discovered this and created merry hell. In the end the First Mate had to conduct a search of the ship to recover the goods as they refused to let us go any further through the canal until they got either the goods or the money. They got their goods back. However, we wanted nothing more to do with them and stopped their 'nice little earner' by lowering our own lifeboat to go ashore.

H.M.R.T. 'Assiduous' steering the Dry Dock A.F.D. 30 through the Suez canal while the large Canal Company tug towed it.

Ismailia is a small town with mainly unpaved roads which were all sand. There was a riding stable which quite a few of the crew used. They had never ridden horses before but used to hire these Arab stallions out and go charging around the town on them. Uniformed sailors look quite of place riding horses!

There was a good sized Forces Club on the southern side of the lake. It was mainly for the use of the Army but they allowed us in also. A good sandy beach and safe swimming was always welcome here.

One unfortunate facility in the town was that of a tattooist. Some of the younger first trippers decided to have tattoos done by this Arab who held shop in a little corrugated iron shed. Without exception all their tattoos turned septic and the inks ran. They were scarred for life.

We eventually got away again and towed the dock through to Suez where the Canal tugs left us. We then headed off down the Gulf of Suez to the Red sea. By now it was so hot 140 deg. F in the engine room that the Third Engineer and I, who stood watch together, used to sit out on deck chairs by the engine room hatch. We could easily see and hear what was going on down below and I used to go down the ladder every 20 minutes or so for a look around and feel the bearings. The tow rope used to slide from side to side over the towing bars above our heads which was a bit disconcerting, but it was a lot better than staying in the stifling heat down below.

On the second day out a severe gale sprang up. This was a surprise to me as I did not expect to encounter gales in the Red Sea of all places, but the weather can be just as changeable here as anywhere else. Because of the gale the Third and I were both down in the engine room when, about 2 a.m. we heard a tremendous 'crack' as the towing wire snapped and the engines suddenly started racing away. The third made a dive for the governor to lower the speed before we ran the bearings out of her. We were surprised to have no instructions from the bridge so the third rang them up. They did not even know the tow wire had snapped. Once we told them, all hell broke loose. All hands were piped on deck. The Skipper took over the bridge. The Mate and Bos'un had all hands down on the after deck to get the tow wire and rope in. This was no joke in rough seas at night. We had been towing on about 1500ft.of 6" wire with another 500 ft. of 16" Manilla rope in the middle. Unlike the Samsonia', the 'Assiduous' did not aspire to the luxury of a towing winch and all this wire and rope had to be manhandled in on the capstan on the after deck.

A soaking wet 16" rope takes a lot of handling, not to mention the 1500 ft. of 6" wire with waves crashing over you all the time. Once the rope was in, it had to be unshackled from the rest of the wire which was then also manhandled on the Capstan until the frayed end came aboard.

It is all very well handling a dry 16" rope in a calm sea, but try a wet rope on a pitching deck with seas crashing over you! Especially in winter in the North Atlantic.

Meanwhile, the Dry Dock, with its skeleton crew of about 10 aboard, was adrift in the gale and could be seen tossing about all over the place.

Our Bosun had the unenviable task of splicing a heavy metal eye piece into the frayed end of the broken 6" wire. When this was eventually done we had to manoeuvre alongside the bow end of the dock and fire a rocket line over for them to catch. They had to stand in the bottom of the dock which was shipping heavy seas right through it. Two men lost their lives during this operation when they were swept overboard. Our line was eventually caught and the Capstan , which had been specially installed on the dock for the voyage , was used to haul it in. Eventually under the most horrendous conditions they managed to secure our wire again.

Floating Dry Dock A.F.D. 30 adrift in a Red Sea gale.

(Photo taken by the author with a Box Brownie camera and developed and printed aboard at the time)

H.M.R.T. 'Assiduous' coming round to re-connect the towrope.

We had to take up the slack very gingerly and just try to ride out the gale. We could not tow her in this weather but we had to try to at least hold her and prevent her being blown ashore as happened to the 'Hesperia's' dock in Libya.

We had hardly got settled down again when 'crack' the wire parted again. All that work and effort was for nothing. We had to start all over again. In fact, believe it or not, we snapped the wire and rope five times in all during the next 24 hours. On two occasions, when trying to re-connect, we hit the dock very hard. We stove in one of our lifeboats and damaged the bulwarks. It then transpired that the Captain and Chief Engineer were drunk. There was a hell of a row between the Officers. The crew, led by the Petty Officers complained bitterly and insisted the First Mate take over the ship. The Captain and Chief had been fermenting the oranges and grapefruits we bought in Haifa and were making their own 'hooch'. Certainly it appeared as though the Captain could endanger the ship and the dry dock, not to mention the lives of those on board.

The Mate locked the Captain in his cabin and took over. Eventually after a couple of days the gale subsided. In response to our radio call for help an ex German tug the 'Josephine Moller' left Port Tewfik to come to our assistance. The two of us then towed the Dry Dock into Port Sudan for repairs. We remained there for 3 weeks.

Port Sudan was a dreadful place. The dry air had no humidity at all and the sun scorched down like a white hot ball. You dare not expose your skin for more than a few minutes. There was nothing for us to do there. There was no Naval Pay Office and quite a few of the ships stores mysteriously disappeared as bit by bit some currency appeared on board. All we could do when we did go ashore was sit in the shade on the verandah of some café in the one main street and gorge on ice creams. Like Port Said, the beer was undrinkable, especially in this climate. The local British Consulate and various ex patriots who represented different company's out here did lay on a couple of parties for us during our three week stay, and they let us use their swimming pool on some occasions. Other than that, we could not wait to get away again.

When we did go, we only went 300 miles down the coast to Massawa in Eritrea. The Moller tug was still assisting us. We anchored off outside the harbour of this ex Italian Naval Base while taking in our ropes and wires. It was mid morning. The Moller tug had a Royal Navy Warrant Officer aboard and he was standing on the stern supervising the incoming wire when it suddenly broke. It whipped round his legs and dragged him over the side of the ship. He managed to get free and surfaced, while a small boat from the port which was luckily alongside was able to rescue him. Unfortunately The fact that for some reason he was wearing rubber thigh boots had actually saved the leg inside the boot.

When the Italians capitulated in this part of the world the Royal Navy had taken over this base and fortunately a hospital had been set up here to which the poor chap was quickly whisked away. It looked as though he had lost his leg only months before he was due for retirement after a lifetime in the Royal Navy. It just goes to show how quickly serious accidents can happen, particularly in towing and salvage work. Once our tow wire was in we proceeded into harbour. The first thing that hit us was the intense heat and high humidity. It was only 300 miles from Port Sudan yet the change in humidity was amazing. The temperature was usually around 130 F. in the shade. And the sweat just rolled out of you.

It was decided we would boiler clean again while in the dockyard, so we were here for a few days. We found the heat to be murderous. We even sweated while swimming in the sea. It was just impossible to cool off. My bunk used to get saturated with sweat to the extent that my mattress squelched as I turned over. Dehydration was a big problem in Massawa and those based ashore used to get a weeks leave in every five to go up to the Capitol, Asmara. We were given 7 days leave there ourselves while the boiler cleaning went on.

SYRIA
CYPRUS
LEBANON
IRAQ
Sea
ISRAEL
Dumyat
Rashid
Port Said
Isma'iliya
JORDAN
Tanta
El Giza
EL QAHIRA (CAIRO)
KUWAIT
El Faiyum
Beni Suef
Beni Mazar
Samalut
El Minya
Mallawi
Asyut
Sohag
SAUDI
ARABIA
Girga
Qena
Luxor
Isna
Kom Ombo
Aswan
TROPIC OF CANCER
Red Sea
Halaib
Wadi Halfa
Port Sudan
Suakin
Tokar
Abu Hamed
Dongola
Karima
Merowe
Ed Debba
Atbara
Ed Damer
Shendi
ERITREA
Agordat
Massawa
Khartoum North
Omdurman
Khartoum
Kassala
Asmara
YEME
Wad Medani
SUDAN
Sennar
El Obeid
Kosti
Gedaref
Gonder
Assab
Aden
Gulf o
Weldiya
DJIBOUTI
Djibouti
Bahir Dar
Dese
Kadugli
Berbera
Debre Mark'os
Malakal
ADIS ABEBA
(ADDIS ABABA)
Dire Dawa
Harer
Hargeysa
ETHIOPIA
Wau
Jima
Asela
Rumbek
Bor
Tambura
Juba

What a relief! Asmara is situated 10,000 feet up in the mountains and 100 miles away. We were told to take our blue uniforms with us as it would be a lot colder up there. A small electric train took us up, winding its way around the barren mountain rocks that shimmered in the heat. Occasionally a few small peasant shanties would be seen but little else. When we reached Asmara we could not believe our eyes. Having travelled through the most primitive of areas we suddenly came into a large modern City built by the Italians. The temperature was like a good English summer. Blossomed trees lined the wide avenues, we could have been in Italy judging by the buildings and weather.

Our crew stayed together in the Hotel, Albergo d'Italia . A medium sized hotel that did us very proud. We had delicious Espresso coffee with cream every morning. Cream cakes were also supplied with it. In the evenings we went out on the town and had 7 course dinners. These always started off with a huge plate of Spaghetti which had to be eaten quickly we were told. After a lot of fun, most of us mastered the correct way to eat it by twisting around one prong of a fork into the bowl of a spoon.

We always drank with our meals and this was invariably a Champagne type of drink. Probably Asti Spumante . Anyway, it was very palatable and only cost five shillings a bottle. By the end of every evening the table, and floor beneath it was littered with empty bottles and we were quite happy.

It was a most enjoyable leave in a very pleasant city. We did not look forward to going back to Massawa at the end of the week, but all good things come to an end.

When we got back to the ship she was ready for us to continue with our tow to Aden and we sailed again the next day. We were glad to get out to sea. Although unbearably hot still, particularly in the engine room and our cabins, at least we had a little relief from the high humidity in Massawa.

Aden had always been a bunkering port for ships on their way to India, the Far East and Australia. In the old days there was a thriving trade for the locals with passengers and crew.

The coal burning ships of old spent quite a time bunkering under the most horrendous sweat shop conditions. Nowadays it is nearly all oil. The ship ties up to a buoy in the middle of the harbour to which is permanently attached an oil pipe line from storage tanks ashore and bunkers are taken in a couple of hours.

The harbour is surrounded by high barren, rocky, mountains from which the sun reflects mercilessly down. There is no sign of any greenery anywhere apart from Jupps Gardens on the sea front which were artificially created. It was a miracle if it ever rained in Aden. You could sit out in the shade of these trees in the gardens and hope to get any semblance of breeze that might blow off the water. Even that was hot.

We wondered how long we might be in Aden and where the next part of our voyage may take us! After about 4 days in port, I was ashore with some other members of the crew when we suddenly heard the urgent recall signal from our ships siren. The whistle kept blowing so we had no choice other than to dash down the steps and get the boat back aboard. It turned out that a large oil tanker had gone aground in the Straits of Perim, the narrow exit from the Red Sea into the Indian Ocean. We had been asked to try and tow her afloat again. We found her undamaged and apparently stuck fast on a sandy bottom. We could not get near enough to fire a rocket line across because of the shallow water, so we had to lower our motor lifeboat and carry a long thin line over. She then hauled in our main tow wire on her capstan. We pulled for all we were worth but no sign of movement. We had to wait about 8 hours for high tide and then work her from side to side for quite a while before she came off. Once released, she was able to continue under her own power so we returned to Aden.

Two or three more days elapsed before we got a job. We had to tow two floating cranes to Karachi in Pakistan. This was a most awkward tow, one behind the other. We prayed for calm seas which we mostly got, but we had a couple of dodgy days when the cranes careered all over the place. We had to keep our speed down to about 2 knots maximum. To travel along the southern coast of the Arabian Peninsular in the steaming heat at only 2 knots was unbearable. We could get no wind down the ventilators.

It took us a few days to get to Karachi . The busy oil tanker shipping lanes across the Straits of Hormuz were a particular hazard for us as well as the tankers. We could not manoeuvre out of their way as we crossed their paths. However- we finally got there. Another successful tow completed.

We were greeted with a wonderful sight as we entered the huge harbour area. There was a magnificent red sunset and literally thousands of small fishing boats with their triangular Lateen sails all over the place. The surrounding land was very flat and difficult to see. The water was as smooth as glass and the whole scene unforgettable.

We handed over the two cranes to small harbour tugs who took them to their ultimate destinations. We tied up to a jetty somewhere which seemed to be out in the wilderness. We were allowed ashore the next day and found we had to get a bus some 5 miles to the City of Karachi. This bus rattled along dusty unpaved roads. It had no windows or sides to it. People were sitting on the roof. The heat, dust and smells were horrible, not to mention the continuously bumpy ride!

Had I known what was in store, I would not have bothered going but it was a first visit to the Indian Sub-continent. My memory is of streets of open shops. Wares were sold on the pavements, such as they were. People and traffic solidly blocked the streets. Bicycle bells were trying to compete with car and bus horns as to who could make the most noise. Among all this throng roamed the Sacred Cows. I think my main memory of the place was to wonder how quickly I could get back aboard my ship!

Fortunately we wasted no more time in Karachi. We sailed again the next day, apparently back to Aden again. This was disappointing as we had thought we might be heading south to Bombay or even Colombo in Ceylon. Before we got to Aden though, our orders were changed. We were to go back to Massawa for another boiler clean. Whereas we dreaded the thoughts of Massawa again, rumour was rife that we would get another leave up in the mountains of Eritrea in Asmara. This was not to be. A quick three days for boiler cleaning, and then the ship was off again. Where she went, I know not! I never went with her. I had developed a very painful Haemerroid condition and, on reporting sick to the Naval Hospital was immediately admitted for what would probably be an operation. So be it! I was glad to find the hospital ward was air conditioned. I suffered my condition for another couple of days before the Surgeon decided to try and cure me with injections. The climate in Massawa was not conducive to a good recovery from operations if they could be avoided therefore they were if at all possible. The injections thankfully worked, but I stayed in the hospital another week while they kept a check that I would have no recurrence.

I was pleased to find the Warrant Officer who had lost his leg when dragged overboard on the 'Josephine Moller' was still in the hospital. I was even more pleased to find out he had not lost his leg. It had been completely severed alright and the Surgeon Captain in charge said there was no more they could do. However, fortunately for him there was a young Surgeon Lieutenant in the hospital at the time who thought he could join the bone and sew the leg back on again. The Warrant Officer was all for it and pleas to the Captain were successful as was the operation. His leg would never grow back to its normal size, and he would always walk with a limp, but at least he had kept his leg.

After this week of observation on me, I was getting a bit bored kicking my heels around the hospital. I discovered there were three other chaps going to Asmara on leave and asked if I could go with them. Permission was granted so, I was very lucky in getting another weeks leave in this beautiful city.

When I returned I was told that a passage had been booked for me to Colombo. The next day I boarded the sleek looking Hunt Class Destroyer H.M.S. 'Cavendish'. She was on her way out east with her two sister ships H.M.S. 'Cavalier' and the Flotilla leader H.M.S. 'Caeser'. This looked exciting I thought! I had never been aboard such a ship before. I was issued with a hammock and taken down to the stokers mess. I had never used a hammock before, all my ships had bunks. My new messmates were incredulous when I did not know how to sling it and wondered what sort of ships I had been on. I must say, I found it the most comfortable way to sleep at sea I had ever known.

HMS Cavendish (Hunt Class Destroyer)

Catering was by the Canteen messing system. Each mess was allowed so much money per day for food. The members of the mess decided what they wanted from a list of ships stores provided. They prepared the vegetables etc., and took the food to the galley where the cooks cooked it. They fed very well. I found mushy peas to be the favourite. They were cheap and needed no preparing. Steamed duff and custard was also popular, no doubt for its filling qualities. The idea was that, if you could feed cheaper than the allowance the balance of the cash was shared out among the mess. There was always a balance for share out!

I was no sooner aboard than we sailed. The three ships kept in line ahead behind the leader H.M.S. 'Caesar'. An economical cruising speed of 20 knots was adopted. I had never sailed at this sort of speed before. It amazed me that the Dolphins could still swim back and forth across the bows as we cut through the water.

Once in the Indian Ocean it was decided to have a gunnery practice. As a passenger with nothing to do I was ordered to keep out of the way below decks while this was going on. I could look out of a porthole though and watched the firing practice of the other ships while having to place my hands over my ears as our own 4.5" guns went off with a tremendous crack.

It was a thrilling and enjoyable trip to Colombo, all the more so as the Captain announced over the loud speakers that the Germans had surrendered and the war in Europe was over when we were half way to Colombo. May 8th. 1945! A day to remember. While great rejoicing was going on in Britain though, there were many of us that still had the dreadful thought of still having the Japanese to contend with. At least the fleet had orders to 'Splice the Mainbrace' on that day. So a double tot of Rum was enjoyed by all.

I was put ashore at Colombo and found they had recently had an air raid from a Japanese aircraft carrier. Ships had been sunk in the harbour , quite a lot of damage done ashore and many killed. I was back in the war zone again!

A Naval truck took me to the barracks about 3-4 miles inland. This was called H.M.S. 'Mayina'. It was a large collection of wooden huts set around an even larger dust bowl of a parade ground. In the Monsoon rains the place became a quagmire.

Colombo was full of interesting things. The wood and Ivory carvings in the shops were marvellous, as was the wonderful jewellery. Beautiful Green Emeralds and Red Rubies were everywhere, made up in to the finest necklaces, bracelets and rings.

There was a fine beach with safe swimming and a service mans club about 4 miles along the coast road. This was called Mount Lavinia and was a very popular visiting place for sailors ashore.

One day a notice was placed on the board saying a trip was being organised to the Capital, Kandy, in the middle of the island. This was to see the annual procession of Elephants carrying the Sacred Tooth of Buddah through the streets to the Temple. It was known as the Perehera. I put my name down for this and, when the appointed day arrived about 20 of us piled into the back of an American Army Dodge truck and off we went.

The journey through lush green jungle and scenic hills was wonderful. As we got further inland we were climbing higher and higher, nearing what is known as Adams Peak. The road was very steep and narrow. We suddenly came to a sharp U-bend with a stone built bridge right on it. There was a sheer precipice to the right hand side. The lorry had to make very small reversals about 12 times to get round this bend. It had air brakes which hissed with every touch. We, sitting in the back and looking down the precipice, were terrified the brakes would fail, or the truck go too far! We made it of course and carried on to the beautiful City of Kandy high in the hills and with a wonderful climate compared to the humid heat of Colombo.

We found a restaurant where most of us enjoyed the usual Curry and Rice. I found curry to be very good for cooling you down in the hot climates. It got dark quite early and, no sooner had we finished our meal than we heard noises in the street. The procession was coming. We were lucky enough to find good vantage points among the thousands of people lining both sides of the main street in Kandy. The procession was led by 'whip crackers'. These men had very long whips which they swished across the road with a loud cracking noise. Woebetide anyone who encroached beyond the pavement! Next to come were the Kandian Dancers. These men and women were dressed overall in exotic brass costumes and headdresses and performed very ancient dances as they progressed along the street. Music was provided by a variety of strange instruments including very long horns.

Kandian Dancers

Huge Elephants followed, each one dressed overall in the most exotic gold embroidered braids with real Gem stones adorning their heads and trunks. The Mahouts sitting on their necks and guiding them were also dressed in beautiful bejewelled clothes and Turbans. The magnificently dressed Feudal Lords walked beside their own Elephants. Interspersed with all this were other exotic dancers and colourfully dressed people, many of who carried flaming torches.

In the middle of this long procession came the Elephant carrying the Sacred Tooth of Buddha. A huge and magnificent beast, it was again dressed in the most exotic style, with what must have been a small fortune in Jewellery draped all over it. A bejewelled 'Howdah' on its back carried the Sacred Tooth in a glass walled case. I have never seen such a magnificent procession in all my life, and felt very privileged that I had 'been in the right place at the right time 'to be able to see it!

The Elephant carrying the Sacred Tooth of Buddha.

The Elephant entering the temple with the Sacred Tooth of the Buddha.

It was 1 a.m. when we left Kandy for the return journey to Colombo. We had downed a few of the local beers by then, which was just as well as the thought of negotiating that bend at Adams Peak again , at night, and going downhill did not bear thinking about! Our young driver was up to it though and did a magnificent job. The only thing to spoil the expedition occurred when we were about 4 miles short of our destination. The heavens opened up and we got drenched on the open backed lorry. We then got a puncture and it was decided the heavy wheel could not be changed in such conditions. We walked the rest of the way in a Monsoon downpour.

It was quite by chance I discovered the Tug Service had recently set up an office in Colombo. More and more tugs were coming out for the far east war. I decided to pay a visit and try to find out where H.M.R.T. 'Assiduous' was and how much longer I was likely to remain in the barracks. Imagine my surprise when I walked in the office and found one of my old skippers, Commander Archibald Leckie of the Samsonia in charge. Ever the opportunist, I decided to take advantage of our past acquaintance and told him that I was most disappointed to have left the 'Assiduous' as I was in line for promotion to Petty Officer and seemed to have now lost that opportunity. He straight away said "That could be overcome. One of the American built Diesel Electric tugs, H.M.R.T. 'Cheerly', was in Mombasa and needed a Stoker P.O. Leave it with me "he said, "and report back in a couple of days". I did that, but he decided that, as I had not been with Diesel Electric before, and as my old ship was due back in Trincomalee in a few days, it would be better if I returned to her. However, he said, the Stoker P.O. is due to return home for demob and you can take his place. I was elated at my sudden promotion, though a bit disappointed that I was going back to the intense heat and humidity of the 'Assiduous'.

Meanwhile I returned to barracks to await my ships return to port. I went to the regulating office and showed them my Certificate of Promotion and was moved to the Petty Officers quarters and mess. My new found promotion brought a few extra perks but all was not to be roses!

It had been decided that a 'Victory in Europe' celebration would be held in Colombo and the main thrust of this would be a March Past around Galle Face Green. Admiral Lord Louis Mountbatten, C in C Far East and {Pacific would come down from his H.Q. in Delhi to take the salute. Once this was known, the organisers decided that the Royal Navy, being the predominant force in Ceylon at that time, would lead the procession. Not only would they lead it, but about 30 Petty Officers would form the front ranks. Dress would be white duck uniforms with belts, boots and gaiters. I told the G.I. I had no boots. He asked me my size and found me a pair within half an hour.

We spent a week drilling on the large dusty parade ground at H.M.S. 'Mayina' under the baking hot sun, much to the amusement of the lower ratings! Mind you, they were also being put through their paces.

It fell upon me, as the tallest Petty Officer in the barracks at that time, to take the lead as the left hand Marker and lead the whole procession.

Came the big day, we all lined up on Galle Face Green, a magnificent large area by the sea. The dominant feature was the Galle Face Hotel in the centre. A large hotel built in Victorian times. Inside were large Marble halls surrounded by mirrors huge chandeliers hung from the high white and gold ceilings and a general air of great opulence abounded within it.

We arrived on the green at about 8 a.m. to get ready for the march off at 10 a.m. It was a magnificent procession taking 2 hours to pass the saluting base. Navy, Army, Air Force and Nurses from all over the commonwealth took part. I felt very proud to be leading such a sight. The only problem I had, and it was a very big one to me, was what do I do when I get out of earshot of one band and into another and find we are marching ' out of step' to the new band! Did I change step or didn't I ? I imagined the whole procession having to change step if I did and fortunately decided the spectacle would be too great to bear! I mentioned my dilemma to the G.I. after the parade and I need not tell you what he would have done to me if I had changed step !!!

Two or three days later I was told that my old ship H.M.R.T. 'Assiduous' was in Trincomalee, the large harbour and Naval Base on the North Eastern coast of Ceylon. I was told to pack my bags ready for an early start the next day. A lorry took myself and several other naval personnel down to Colombo railway station. A carriage had been reserved for us, which was just as well as people were clambering all over the train which included such things as live chickens etc.

The seats on the train were wooden slats so the journey was not taken in the utmost of comfort! The windows were all wide open because of the heat and humidity, so the smoke and grit from the ancient steam locomotive pulling us would often come into the carriage. The journey took about 8 hours and, if I remember rightly we were given a 'packed lunch' which consisted of little more than a couple of corned beef sandwiches. We were pestered at all the many stops to buy Bananas. These were of the small sweet type grown locally. They were very tasty and we bought them by the hand. About 20 at a time. The only problem was they gave us all ' the runs!'. For drinks we could only get Lemonade made from powder.

The journey through the jungle and heartland of Ceylon was interesting. Small villages of reed huts often emerged through jungle clearings. Elephants were seen working at various tasks. Large modern Planters houses stood out in relief on the hillsides. However, the journey was long, hot uncomfortable, and eventually became tedious. We were more than pleased when we arrived at Trincomalee at about 4 p.m.

A naval lorry was waiting for the train and took those of us joining ships down to the jetty where picket boats would take us out into the harbour where a massive collection of ships were at anchor. This long wooden jetty is well known to all sailors who have visited this port as "Pepperpot Jetty". Why? I have no idea.

About 10 of us were standing on the jetty, way out in the open, waiting for our ships picket boats to come and collect us, when suddenly the heavens opened up and we all got thoroughly drenched to the skin in the heavy Monsoon rain which came down like a solid wall of water. One by one my companions boats came and off they went. Finally I was the only one left. I could see the 'Assiduous' anchored way out but there was no sign of activity where the ships boat was concerned. I wondered whether they knew I was here or not! I asked the last boat that left to signal them for me. Apparently they did as, after a 2 hour wait in the pouring rain my boat finally came. They had NOT been expecting me.

My old shipmates were very surprised to see me back again, and more so when they found out I was replacing Bill Humphreys, the Stoker Petty Officer. Bill of course was more than pleased to be relieved to go home for demobilisation. I moved in with the Bosu'n with whom I shared a two berthed cabin on the Starboard side. We also had a separate mess room shared with the other three P.O.'s aboard, the Chief Cook, Chief Steward and Carpenter.

I found that the Chief Engineer had been put ashore sick and no replacement found for him. This meant that I had to take the 8-12 watch below as the Engineer. I was an Engineer at last, in practice if not rank and qualification.

Palk Strait
Kankesanturai
Point Pedro
Sri Lanka
Palk Bay
Jaffna
100 km
100 miles
Mullaittivu
Mankulam
Mannar I.
Mannar
Gulf of Mannar
Vavuniya
Yan Oya
Trincomalee
Bay of Bengal
Anuradhapura
Kantalai
Kalpitiya
Kala Oya
Kathiraveli
Puttalam
Polonnaruwa
Maho
Batticaloa
Mahaweli Ganga
Chilaw
Matale
Kurunegala
Kandy
Amparai
Negombo
Gal Oya
Kegalla
Kelani Ganga
Colombo
Badulla
Dehiwala
Kotte
Pottuvil
Moratuwa
Moneragala
Panama
Panadura
Kalu Ganga
Walawe Oya
Ratnapura
Kalutara
Opanake
Kirinda
Hambantota
Ambalangoda
Galle
Matara

CEYLON

CHAPTER EIGHT

Another invasion in the offing !

The huge harbour at Trincomalee was packed solid with a wide variety of ships, rather reminiscent of those days in Southern England prior to the Normandy invasion. The largest of these was the magnificent looking French Battleship Cardinal Richelieu. It was quite obvious that something was afoot and we could only guess that an invasion of Malaya was about to begin. Sure enough, a couple of days later we all sailed heading east.

The Bay of Bengal was flat calm, the surface of the sea shimmering like glass. The heat and humidity was almost unbearable and temperatures in the 'Assiduous' engine room reached 140 degrees. We had a landing craft LCT break down and request a tow while their engineer tried to repair the fault. This we duly did. It was not long before another one had a similar problem, then a third. We had two astern and one either side of us before we twigged they were skiving for an easy trip across and thought they were on to a good thing !

The French Battleship Cardinal Richelieu.
(Note the quadruple gun turrets)

Apparently we were headed for the Malacca Straits and Malaya. The invasion would take place about half way up the Peninsula in the area just south of Penang. Port Swettenham, Port Dixon and Port Love. The Richelieu and heavy cruisers would go on ahead to 'soften up' the target area. Two Aircraft carriers were due to join us to provide air cover. We knew of the hard fight the Japanese were capable of putting up and wondered what would be in store for us here !

I suppose we were about half way across the Bay of Bengal when we got the news! The Atom Bomb had been dropped on Hiroshima. Later another one on Nagasaki. Then the Japanese unconditionally surrendered. We praised the good Lord for that! Speed was put on to get to Malaya as soon as possible. A lot of ships were re-routed to Penang and others went straight on down to Singapore.

The Japanese Surrender party aboard the Battleship USS Missouri in Tokyo Bay.

We spent about three weeks around the Port Swettenham area, doing the odd towing job, but mostly lying at anchor and getting rather bored. Landing and supply ships were discharging cargoes and personnel here as Penang was pretty well congested. We were really just standing by in case any of the ships broke down or could not get themselves off the beach again.

Most of our days were spent swimming while at anchor but we always had to have a good lookout on the bridge for sharks. Almost as deadly were the large 'Man o' War' jellyfish which could give a lethal sting from their very long tentacles.

Local natives used to come out to us in their Prahu's, small canoes with outriggers. They brought large Pineapples which they would trade to us for as little as one cigarette. Not having seen pineapples at home since before the war we went for them in a big way. We just peeled them and ate them like ordinary apples, the juice running all down you as you ate.

Along with a few other members of the crew I started getting quite severe earache. We reported sick and were taken to a nearby hospital ship at anchor. It turns out that there is a microscopic organism in these waters that attacks the inner ear giving quite severe pain. Drops of some kind were given us and the condition soon cleared up thank goodness. We had quite enough to contend with aboard Assiduous without this sort of thing. Of course it put an end to our swimming!

Came the day, we received orders to sail to Batavia (now Djakarta) the Capital of Java. We went off on our own but with some concern as we were very short of food and cigarettes and were unable to get supplies before leaving. We had been living rather badly as it was and now many of us were suffering from 'Prickly Heat', an irritating, sore and painful rash. One or two came out with severe and very painful boils, the third Engineer suffering particular agony with these. By the time we got to Batavia we were living on absolutely nothing other than boiled rice and tinned tomatoes. Not a piece of bread, biscuit or anything else was on board. We were also desperately short of water for drinking, washing and the ships boiler. For some reason we could not even get any water in Batavia at that time.

We had to put the third Engineer ashore to have his boils treated at the local Hospital. The poor man was in desperate agony. Later we received a terrible shock when we heard he had been shot dead by a sniper. We were to find a lot more trouble before we left Java. The Javanese were determined not to let the ruling Dutch back into their Island. They wanted their Independence.

The loss of the third engineer meant there was only the second and myself to keep an engine room watch and the two of us had to work 6 hours on and 6 hours off. Under these conditions of heat, humidity and loss of diet this became very debilitating indeed.

We were ordered to escort three LCT landing craft and two MFV's along the north coast of Java to the port of Semerang. We did our best to catch water from the monsoon rains which came down twice a day. We made a hole in the canvas awning over the boat deck and ran a hose pipe down to the water tank. This was not nearly enough to satisfy our thirsty boiler though. Mind you, it was very good to be able to stand on deck and have a good shower in the pouring rain.

Upon reaching Semerang we left the LCT's and MFV's and were ordered to sail further along the coast to the large port and one time Dutch Naval Base of Surabaya. We were told we would meet up with a landing force coming down from Singapore on the way.

It so happens our only Radio Officer was not keeping a night watch (The poor chap had to sleep sometimes!) and unknown to us therefore the landing force had been delayed by 24 hours. We arrived at the 40 mile long 'roads' that led down to Surabaya and found two Japanese Destroyers anchored there. They signalled to warn of a minefield on the way, and trouble ashore with the Indonesians. We were now doing the 'unthinkable' and pumping salt water into the boiler. We had no other choice. We told the Japs we had to go in for water. They showed us a path through the minefield. The skipper, as eccentric as he was, ordered the Battle Ensign to be flown, and thus we charged down the ' roads' to Surabaya, pumping sea water into the boiler, and streaming thick black smoke from our funnel. (I wonder if any other tug ever flew that ensign!) Before reaching the docks we found a line of blockships had been sunk across the channel. There was a small gap in the middle, enough for one ship to pass through. One side of the gap had the old Dutch battleship Van Tromp sunk to deck level.

Typical scenery when sailing round the many Islands in the Indonesian Archipelago. One of the hundreds of Volcanoes.

Further on we rounded a bend and suddenly came in sight of the docks. Large warehouses along the quay had the Red & White flag of the Indonesian Republic painted on their sides. Big letters proclaimed "Long Live the Indonesian Republic" and "Down with Dutch Imperialism". A fearsome looking piece of artillery was pointing at us as we approached the quayside. We were told by someone with a loud hailer to anchor out in the harbour. We replied that we were desperate for water and were coming alongside. The gun fired a shot across our bows. We anchored! Later a small motor launch approached us. It was crowded with Javanese men dressed in Japanese Officers uniforms, complete with swords. We were asked if there were any Dutchmen aboard? We replied "No", upon which they insisted on coming aboard.

They lined all our crew up on deck and inspected us closely. Whether they had a way of telling a Dutchman from an Englishman I do not know! Had there been any Dutch on board they would have been taken away to a prison camp and possible execution.

Eventually they left us, but still would not let us alongside for water. We remained at anchor that night with a searchlight playing on us. We kept a very wary eye on that large gun still pointing at us.

The next morning two very smart looking British Destroyers arrived. They were the advance guard of the main landing force. They were very surprised to find us here and apparently signalled back to Lord Mountbattens H.Q. "Arrived in Surabaya as ordered and found it occupied by one of His Majesty's Rescue Tugs". The Senior Naval Officer came over to ask us what the situation was. We told him of our experience and I suppose he went away to think what to do next.

Later in the day other ships started arriving, including troopships with Indian soldiers of the Mahratta Regiment on board. All anchored off. We eventually received a signal from the N.O.I.C. "Suggest as you were here first, you up anchor and make to go alongside and see what happens. Our guns are trained on that artillery piece ashore". Obviously a mere tug was 'expendable' if necessary!

We weighed anchor and went alongside the quay. We were closely questioned again. Were they Dutch aboard all those ships out there? We truthfully said "No". I think the Destroyers guns must have impressed them a little! They left us alone alongside the quay.

The next thing we knew was the two merchant ships coming alongside . There was not a soldier in sight. Once alongside the quay though a great clanging was heard as the ships bulwarks, which were hinged, dropped down. Gangplanks were laid to the quay and the troops rushed ashore fanning out in all directions as they secured the docks in no time at all.

Once the docks were secured, I went ashore to search for water. I found the mains, but also found them dry. The water had been cut off. I eventually discovered a water barge that was fully loaded and thought our troubles would be over. The barge was driven by a large Caterpillar diesel engine. After about an hour I managed to get it started and, with the assistance of two or three of the deck crew, started to sail it proudly round to our ship. It was not to be though. The engine suddenly seized up. It had been sabotaged with sand in the fuel tank. We managed to get a line ashore and winched the barge alongside the dock. Later we lowered the ships motor lifeboat and towed it round alongside us and pumped our tanks full.

Meanwhile the rest of the crew had been foraging around in the warehouses looking for food. They only found more rice, which we duly helped ourselves to. But then, a miracle happened! We found large wooden cases piled high to the roof of the warehouse and inside them were millions of cigarettes and cigars. We had been smoking tea leaves wrapped up in any paper we could find, also dried weed off the ships hull. We were about ready to cut each others throats for a cigarette!

We found two kinds of cigarettes in these cases, both Japanese Military issue. They were called Semengats. The officers were wrapped in silver paper the troops in very ordinary cheap paper. They tasted awful by our standards but we were very glad to get them. The cigars were wonderful. The wooden boxes were lead lined to keep them fresh. We loaded the ship with all we could carry. Then someone found sacks of 'flour' so we all looked forward to our 'Newfie' cook baking some bread. The 'flour' turned out to be powdered white rubber. Enough said!

We heard that things were going pretty badly with the Javanese. We had managed to get a lot of Dutch families who had survived imprisonment from the Japanese free. They arrived in trucks down at the docks. Mostly women and children, they were in a pitiful state. One of the destroyers laid on a tea party on the quayside for them. The most sickly of them were taken aboard two destroyers and raced off at full speed for Singapore. Others went on one of the troopships.

The Senior Army officer in charge was a Brigadier Mallaby. A fine man standing over 6'tall. I believe he came from an aristocratic family. He wandered along the quay one day and was quite happy to talk to our stokers as well as every one else. He told us there was a problem with the Javanese. We did not want to fight them, especially after all they had gone through with the Japs. We were only there to liberate them, but they did not trust us. They thought we would assist the Dutch to take control again.

One day the Brigadier decided he wanted to talk to the Javanese leader. He went outside the dock area in his care, with only his driver and unarmed. A patrol stopped them on the road and he asked to be taken to their leader. The patrol shot them both dead at point blank range. It was a terrible tragedy. The Mahratta's dearly loved their Brigadier and nearly went berserk when they heard what had happened. The next morning we found many Javanese bodies floating down past our ship.

We finally got orders to sail for Singapore but had hardly left the quayside when the air pump, a large cast iron vacuum pump that works off the main engine, blew up. The whole cylinder cracked all round and water poured through it. We were finished. Since we had left Massawa in the Red Sea from our last boiler clean, the ship had been working solidly with no time for maintenance or repairs. The crew were exhausted from the poor conditions on board. Particularly as we had lived on a diet of boiled rice and tinned tomatoes for nearly three months now. Most of us, including myself, looked as though we had just been released from a Jap prison camp ourselves. We were as skinny as rakes and our ribs stuck out of our bodies.

We were now stuck in Surabaya with no chance of going anywhere. It became a bit disconcerting as the fighting ashore got worse. Some locals had penetrated the docks and caused some damage. The water mains were back on but we did not trust the water for drinking in case it had been 'tampered' with. We had no means of testing it.

It was decided that we would have to leave. Two naval frigates were leaving for Singapore and one of them the "Loch Tarbert" would tow us there. We started off with a side tow and headed for the open sea we were doing a good speed approaching the sunken blockships across the 'roads' when suddenly the bow ropes broke, one after the other, the two ships fanned apart held only by the stern ropes Luckily the Mate took in the situation instantly and dashed down to the after deck, grabbing an axe on the way, and chopped through the stern ropes.

A good weigh was still on our ship as we headed for a collision with the sunken Dutch battleship Van Tromp. The skipper shouted down to those standing on the fore deck taking in the scene to "Drop the Anchor" someone did. We pulled up within inches of the Van Tromp a very narrow escape. Meanwhile "Loch Tarbert", having her engines on full power was able to steer clear once we had severed the stern ropes.

When we hitched up to her again she towed us astern in a more sedate manner. We, of course, felt somewhat embarrassed that, being a deep sea tug we were being towed ourselves. To see us following along in the wake of the frigate was very 'infra dig'! After all, we couldn't be 'pushing' the darn frigate could we?

While on our way to Singapore another problem arose. I complained of a lump under my left arm and loss of proper use. The skipper signalled the frigate who had a Doctor on board. He was asked if I had a red line showing down my arm? To which we replied in the affirmative. He said I had blood poisoning and must go aboard for treatment. I would die if left. They sent a boat over for me. I had great difficulty climbing over the side and boarding this boat with the use of only one arm. However, I managed it in the end and spent the rest of the voyage aboard the frigate where at least I had some comfort and decent food in the ships sick bay. Luckily for the 2nd.Engineer he had no watch to keep, otherwise he would have to have taken the ship all the way without a break.

H.M.S. Loch Tarbert
(Frigate)

We arrived in Singapore about a week before Christmas 1945. By now my arm had been cleared of its poison thank goodness. The frigate transferred me back to Assiduous once we had all docked. We still had no food aboard, but I noticed one of our sister ships alongside the quay further up the docks. I think it was H.M.R.T. 'Griper'. I knew the Chief Steward aboard her, a Londoner named Rawlings. As soon as I could I made my way ashore and went aboard her. He was amazed to see me and when I told him of the sorry state of our food locker he soon rustled me up something to eat. We then drank a bottle of 'Pussers Rum' together while exchanging stories of where we had been and what we had been doing. I finally 'staggered' back aboard 'Assiduous' in the early hours of the morning loaded with all sorts of tinned food and bread.

We were moved into the Keppel Dockyard the next day and went into dry dock for a complete overhaul. At last we were at rest and food and cigarettes came on board. I had developed Ulcers on my legs which were very supurous and would not heal with the continual sweating of my body.

A clean shirt would be saturated within ten minutes of putting it on. I had to go to the naval hospital and have the dressings on my legs renewed every day. I think they used Sulphur powder and bandaged them up. It was over six months later back home in England before they finally healed.

I was absolutely amazed at the skills of the local shipyard workers who were doing our refit. They had only the most primitive of tools by our standards but did a wonderful job. Their pay was derisory, even in those days. I believe the Head Serang only got about 3/6d a day.

I recall asking one of their Carpenters if he would make me a bookshelf for our cabin. In no time at all, and with only an axe to work with, he had carved out scroll like brackets to support the shelf, and the shelf it self, while holding the wood between his toes.

There was little for us to do on board each day, and we had quite a few weeks back pay we could draw on, so we wandered around the town exploring everywhere. It was amazing what was in the shops. The locals had managed to hide many things of pre-war manufacture from the Japanese. I bought a German Zeiss-Ikon Camera. I spent nearly a week bargaining with the shopkeeper before he let me have it for 200 cigarettes. I think he was glad to get rid of me in the end!

I went to the local Theatre one evening and saw John Gielgud playing "Hamlet" and on another night Noel Cowards "Blithe Spirit". Most nights were spent in the Fleet Canteen in Keppel Road though. It was rather too conveniently situated between our dock and the City. Some 2,000 Royal Navy and Merchant Navy sailors used to fill it every night. The beer was a Canadian bottled beer called "Dawes." There was a system of rationing whereby every sailor arriving in Singapore was given only three beer tickets a week. This was obviously pretty useless to thirsty sailors and many soon found a way round it.

I met up with a Royal Marine Transport Group who were based ashore. They had found a Chinese Singaporean who could print these beer tickets for them (they were very easy to forge) and were making a lot of money selling them to all and sundry. The other racket was buying the beer in the Canteen at 75 Straits Cents a bottle and selling it to a very ready market to the taxi drivers outside at $7 a bottle. These chaps were making an awful lot of money and I know of one fellow who managed to get enough of it home to buy a house in Cardiff. I admit to managing to sell a few bottles myself

from tickets provided by the Marines. This helped to finace my stay in Singapore.
Christmas Day 1945 was quite memorable to say the least. My Marine friends had invited me over to their Sergeants Mess for the day. When I arrived at about 10.30 a.m. I found most of them in a state of stupor lying on their beds. A chipped enamel mug of Rum was thrust into my hand and I managed to make this last until lunchtime. Everyone seemed to 'perk up' come lunchtime and were in a party spirit. We had a magnificent traditional Christmas Dinner served to us by the Officers. On board the 'Assiduous' there was little to get excited about!

There was a lot of racketeering and black marketing going on in Singapore after the war. I guess the opportunities were there, and people who had enough of war were quick to seize upon them to their own advantage. Things like Army motorbikes were regularly stolen and spirited away. A couple of lads on my ship (who shall be nameless) stole an Army jeep. They brought it down to the docks. This was quickly painted in Naval Grey and used for the benefit of the ships crew while we were there.

Conditions aboard were still very atrocious. Mess everywhere. The cockroach infestation was horrendous. Now we not only had the European variety but the larger 'Bombay Ducks' that flew around the cabin. You could hear them crack their hard wings as they hit the steel bulkheads. They were into your food and your mouth if you slept with it open. I pleaded sickness, what with my leg ulcers and by now severe dehydration. The M.O. had me transferred to the Naval Barracks that had been set up on Blakang Mati Island just offshore. I was certainly glad to get away from H.M.R.T. 'Assiduous' at last.

I was not bad enough to be excused duties though and, as I held the rank of Stoker Petty Officer I was, in Naval terms a 'Disciplinary P.O.'. I did not realise that only Seamen and Stoker P.O.'s were thus classified and there was a distinct shortage of them in the barracks at that time. I was roped in for duty each day. I found myself on parade at 07.30 hours where I was handed a party of about 80 Japanese prisoners. I was unarmed and alone with these men and had to take them down to the jetty where a landing craft would take us out to cargo ships anchored in the bay. The Japs were used as stevedores to unload the ships. The first thing I learned was that the Japs had to double wherever they went. This meant I had to run with them. No joke in the heat of Singapore and in my state of health! I soon found out why I did not need to be armed though. The Japanese Officers disciplined their own men to such an extent that they beat them mercilessly if they 'stepped out of line' or did not work hard enough. The most senior officer had been the Chief Officer on the heavy cruiser "Myoko" who, along with her sister ship the "Takao" had been the subject of Lt. Frazer and John McGuiness Midget Submarine attack when they won the V.C. for placing limpet mines on their hulls and sinking them in the shallow waters of the harbour.

They were all small men, but I noted, extremely fit and strong. We would board the Merchant ships about 8-8.30 a.m. The derrick operators never started work until 9 a.m. so the Japs would sit around the hatch combings massaging each other. I was amazed at the size and weight of some items they lifted by hand.

I soon got bored of sitting around all day with nothing to do while my charges worked, and started going ashore for the day and leaving them to it, coming back about 4 p.m. to collect them for the return trip to Blakang Mati Island.

My day was not always over when I returned my charges to their camp. As there was a shortage of Seaman and Stoker P.O.'s in the barracks at that time. I was roped in to be in charge of an 8 man Patrol in the Fleet Canteen on 2 or 3 nights a week. I had never done this type of duty before. My men and I were armed with only a long truncheon which I had never been shown how to use, and I was only 20 years old.

My duties were to stop soldiers coming in and stop the beer selling rackets. The trouble was that up to now I had been involved in these rackets myself. My friends of course were sill carrying on as usual, and it was a case of "We're alright tonight lads, 'Lofty' is P.O. of the Patrol!" I was pressed to have a drink at nearly every table so had too much for my own good! On one particular night I was glad I had drunk a few! Some soldiers from the Cameron Highlanders had got into the canteen somehow and, by the time they had a few drinks, had picked a fight with some perfectly legitimate Lascar Merchant Seamen from India. One of my patrol came looking for me to tell me about it and as I ran out into the main entrance to the club I saw the seamen being chased out by the Highlanders. Bottles were flying, boots were being used to kick them and punches were doing a lot of damage to the poor Lascars. Once the soldiers got them down into the Monsoon ditch outside the club they were kicking their heads with army boots.

I came to the ringleader and started tapping him on the head with my truncheon. I dare not hit too hard as I was frightened of cracking his skull. I eventually managed to get one of the seaman out of the ditch and started running him up the road to where I knew there was a Military Police post about 100 yards away. The soldiers gave chase, but I just made the post before they caught up with me. There was still a lot of shouting and scuffling going on. One soldier had a finger bitten almost right through. A Captain in the Military Police came out and gave the soldier a good hard slap round the face and told him to "Shut up". Eventually the scene was calmed down and I had to give a report and what had gone on. It was definitely the soldiers fault. They had come out looking for trouble.

A couple of days later I was ordered to attend at their barracks where they faced a 'court martial' I hated having to give evidence against them but I could only tell the truth about what happened. I do not know what sentences they got. When I returned to my barracks I was asked what went on by our Gunnery Officer in charge. I reported the same to him. I did say that, had I been armed with a revolver I could have fired a couple of shots into the air which I thought would have calmed the situation a lot quicker. I commented that I was frightened to head them any harder on the head in case I cracked their skulls. This brought forth a gasp of amazement! "You actually hit them on the head?" I was asked. "My God man, you are supposed to hit them on the elbow or behind the knees, this will paralyse them from attacking any further". I could only reply that I had never been told this.

Fortunately for me I only had to survive about three weeks of these duties before I was informed that the aircraft carrier H.M.S. 'Victorious' was due in tomorrow and I was to get my kit ready to board her and sail for home as a passenger the next day. This was great news. Both she and the 'Illustrious' were ferrying Naval personnel back home from Sydney, Australia for de-mob. All the ships planes had been put ashore and 2,000 of us were sleeping on small folding canvas beds on the floor of the hanger. The actual trip home was a dream, good food, a great ' Slop Chest' where you could buy very comfortable American made shoes, lengths of Navy Serge material and White Duck as well as many other things. The daily Rum ration had been stopped in the R.N. and there was what they called a 'Goffer Bar' on the flight deck where you could buy soft drinks.

The ships speed amazed me. Nearly 30 knots I was told. I remember sitting on the bow of the flight deck as we approached Colombo and to me it was like being in a car. 'Victorious' took 28 days from Sydney to Plymouth. 21 Days from Singapore to Plymouth and an unbelievable 36 hours from Gibraltar. It was great to be home again, but the first thing to marr my homecoming was to happen as soon as we docked in Plymouth. Naval buses took us to the railway station for our various trains but we were ordered to leave our luggage on the quayside where lorries would pick it up and take it all to the station for us.

I had a Kit Bag and a good suitcase. All my 'treasures' collected at various ports from Malta to Java were in it. Photographs, camera, souvenirs, discharge book and records of my sea going career. Guess what? Some b...... stole the case. Apparently there was a lot of this going on. I lost the lot. I am still heartbroken to this day over the mean so and so who could do such a thing to a returned serviceman! I would have had many more photo's and records to include in this book if it were not for this mean thief!

H.M.S. Victorious – my 'Taxi' home from Singapore after the war.

I was sent to the tugs depot at Harwich first. Then given two weeks leave. On my return I was sent to the Royal Naval Hospital at Gillingham in Kent. I was still in pretty poor shape with leg ulcers and severe dehydration following our experiences in Java. I spent a month there before being finally discharged.

I thought my sea going days were over, but it was not long before I heard the call of the sea once more and I rejoined the Merchant Navy again.

CHAPTER NINE

S.T. SHELBRIT V

The Shelbrit V, as her name implies, was owned by the Shell Oil Co. Ltd., At 1200 tons she was slightly larger than the average coastal tanker and carried a total crew of 16. She had been running backwards and forwards from the great Esso Oil Refinery at Fawley on Southampton Water to Shoreham in Sussex. As I was living in nearby Brighton at the time this sounded like a great opportunity to me, especially as I had been offered the third engineers job on her. I had an excellently furnished cabin to myself on the starboard side and the officers had a well appointed ward room for meals and use as a saloon during the day.

She was run on the lines known as a 'weekly boat'. Like most coasters, the owners provided a Cook/Steward, a galley and a stove plus fuel. The crew all paid the Cook/Steward so much a week as agreed by all, and it was his job to buy all the food when in port and cook it for the crew. At this time 16 of us were paying him 15/- a week (0.75p) each and feeding fairly well. It seems hard to believe as I write that 16 men could all be adequately fed on only £12 a week! But we did.

The ship was sailing on the next tide at about 6 p.m. so I had to hurry back to my lodgings and pack up my gear. I paid for my room until the end of the week and away I went.

Being the Third Engineer my watch was, as always the 12-4 a.m. and p.m. We sailed out through the lock gates at Shoreham soon after 6 p.m. It was only about a 5 hour run down to Fawley so we would be there before my watch was due. I took the opportunity to go below during the Second Engineers watch and familiarise myself with the engine layout and various pumps, valves etc.

It was a calm run down and we dropped anchor off Fawley before midnight. We would go alongside and load Petrol the next morning. We sailed for Shoreham again just after lunch and made the evening tide through the lock gates. I took my first watch and found the job to be an absolute 'doddle'. A fireman looked after the oil fired boiler, and a greaser took care of oiling the main engine and ancilliary's. Apart from answering the telegraph as we entered or left port, I had little to do other than keep a general eye on things. I used to take a book down below to read while on watch.

This would suit me down to the ground I thought! Backwards and forwards to Shoreham, but guess what? The very next trip we filled up at Fawley alright but were sent down to Falmouth to discharge our cargo. This was something I had not foreseen but nevertheless, it made little difference to me where we went, being the freelance that I was.

From Falmouth we went round Lands End and up to Milford Haven on the south west coast of Wales to load at the large Mobil Oil Refinery and then round to the west coast of Ireland where we sailed up the river Shannon to Limerick. We entered the Shannon in the middle of the morning on a large Atlantic swell. Being off watch, I was able to admire the view all around at this majestic spot. There is a small Island called Scattery Island at the mouth of the Shannon and the families living there have been there for generations. They act as the river Pilots and we watched with fascination as a long upturned skinned boat with eight or ten pairs of legs under it came moving down the beach like some large beetle. On reaching the water it was quickly upturned and the carriers jumped straight into it. Oars were immediately put out and the crew rowed with all their might through the surf and into the swell. We then noticed the oars had no blades to them. They were just round poles. This was so they would not 'catch crabs' in the surf and swells that always abound here. The boat was so light in weight that the poles were quite adequate enough to propel them along at a good speed.

These men seemed to be capable of launching and rowing their boat in any weather and had proved their skills over many years. As they came alongside us one of the rowers quickly shipped his oars and, standing up in the wildly bucking boat, leapt aboard us as they rode the crest of a wave. He was to be our Pilot up the Shannon. I must say I found it gratifying to be visiting places I had never been to before once again. It was all part of a sailors life! The Shannon was certainly worth sailing up and the City of Limerick had a charm all of its own. Mind you, I found it most unusual to see so many priests walking around the City. It seemed that nearly every other person I passed was crossing themselves as they passed a priest.

We only spent the night there on this occasion. The thing about tankers, particularly the small coastal ones, is that it does not take long to pump your cargo ashore so you do not get so long in port.

Our Cook/Steward gave notice that he would be leaving us on our return to Milford Haven. We were disappointed as he was quite good. He was a family man though and his home being in Shoreham the previous regular runs had suited him fine. Now he was not getting home at all he did not want to stay. His replacement that we took on in Milford Haven proved to be an absolute disaster. Not only couldn't he cook, he had no idea what to buy or how to cook it. We suffered him for a month before the crew, almost on the point of mutiny, insisted the Skipper get rid of him immediately. We were in Limerick at the time but the skipper sacked him there and then and even paid his passage home.

We 'jumped out of the frying pan and into the fire'. A very large 18 stone Irishman who had been working in the docks applied for the job. He reckoned he had been to sea as a cook before. You could have fooled us! We were sailing that afternoon, in the absence of any other applicant the skipper took him on. We had to pay double that week. The previous incumbent had left no money and nothing in the larder. The new cook had to go ashore and shop before we could sail. He also proved absolutely useless. If anyone complained he adopted a very aggressive attitude and everyone was frightened of him. The last straw came when, after we had suffered him for a week, he gave us our evening meal. One tinned Pilchard on a plate. The crew refused to sail with him any longer. As we sat at the saloon table, I said "Good God, even I could do better than that". Someone said "Why don't you then?" I thought about it for a bit. I liked cooking. It would be a day job so no more night watches to keep. The third engineers job was such a 'doddle' it had become a bit boring. "How about me taking on the job, Captain " I said. The rest all backed me up. When we got back to Limerick again the Irishman was sacked. Once again he adopted a very aggressive attitude towards the crew and threatened to bring a crowd of Limerick dockers down to sort us out. His ranting and raving got so bad that the Garda (Police) had to be called to remove him from the ship and guard us until we sailed again.

Once again there was nothing in the larder. I took two crew members ashore with me to do some shopping and started off with a large leg of lamb to give them a proper roast dinner for a change. Tinned fruit and custard followed.

The galley was small and had a cast iron coal fired range in it. I had to get used to cooking on this but soon found it no problem. We went back to Milford Haven arriving on a Friday and luckily had the weekend in port. On Saturday I got the bus into Pembroke where my first purchase was a good cookery book. I had more or less planned my weeks menu ahead so knew what I wanted to buy. My budget was rapidly running out. I decided to ask the crew for another 1/6d per week putting their keep up to 16/6d. I pointed that there not been an increase for some time. I had already proved that I could cook them a decent meal and promised them better things to come. They all agreed readily.

The first thing I did was to take a leaf out of the Norwegians book from when I was on the old 'Veni'. I had a large cast iron cooking pot and made a split pea soup with a couple of very cheap gammon knuckles in it. This was kept on the galley stove 24 hours a day and the crew could come and help themselves to it whenever they wanted, night or day. This proved very popular, particularly with the deck crews on cold nights. I would replenish the soup every day and, once a week wash out the pot and start all over again varying the content each week. The pea soup always proved the most popular though.

I had nothing to do in the evenings while at sea so I got out my trusty cookery book and taught myself how to make bread, cakes and pastry. I was soon 'up to my elbows' in flour in the evenings. I made some very good bread, cakes and fruit pies, also steak & kidney pies. Good cooking smells started permeating the quarters and the crew were constantly poking their heads through the galley door to ask what I was cooking now.

When we were in the larger ports I used to frequent the dockside pubs and get to know some of the cooks and stewards from the larger deep sea ships. After a drink or two I would plead poverty aboard our ship and more often than not was invited back aboard and given all sorts of goodies. On one occasion we were back in Southampton and I got friendly with a crowd from the 'Queen Elizabeth' who took me back aboard and loaded me with all sorts of delicacies. I was always looking for ways to supplement our menus without further cost. In Pool, Dorset one day, a ship astern of us was unloading potatoes into railway trucks. There was a potato shortage at that time. As the trucks were filled and shunted along the quay they soon came alongside us! Needless to say a few sacks 'mysteriously' found their way aboard the 'Shelbrit V'!

Another time we were in Milford Haven on a wet and miserable Sunday. The pubs never opened on a Sunday in that part of Wales then. The potato shortage was still on and I spied a large field of them growing on the other side of the Sound. It was a very tempting target! I asked some of the crew whether they fancied a bit of lifeboat practice? It was not until I pointed out the object of the exercise that they agreed. Down went the lifeboat, the engine was started and we were soon across the Sound armed with shovels and sacks. We decided that two sacks would be enough and quickly got back aboard before we were discovered. This sort of activity left more money in the kitty to be spent on more luxurious items!

We were pleased we never went back to Limerick again and started going to places like Cork, Dublin, Drogheda and Belfast. Liverpool, Ellesmere Port, Fleetwood and Preston also found there way into our itinerary. Soon we were going even further north to Glasgow, Kyle of Lochalsh and Stornoway up in the Hebrides. Fleetwood was always a useful call. I would be waiting as the deep sea trawlers came in and could usually scrounge a sackful of Cod or Haddock from them.

We fed very well on the Shelbrit V while I was Cook/Steward. I enjoyed the job(and the popularity) How on earth do you do it on 16/6d a week? They would ask. I never let on. I was tempted to ask them for more money, but didn't.

I carried on with this job for about 5 months but then decided I needed a holiday. I also thought I would like to go back deep sea again. It was getting a bit monotonous visiting the same ports over and over again!

The crew were devastated when they heard I was leaving. All sorts of persuasions were offered to make me change my mind. It was very flattering but no, I needed a rest and a change. I left a full larder and some money in the kitty as I left the ship in Swansea and got the train back to Brighton. The crew all knew what I had left and the new chap would have no excuse. In a port like Swansea though, they had a good chance of getting an experienced man.

CHAPTER TEN

ss. Sedgepool
(Sir Robert Ropner & Co. Ltd.,)

ex Wartime Liberty ship " Samdart."

After spending a couple of weeks kicking my heels around Brighton I decided to go down to Southampton one Monday morning and see what sort of ship and job I could get. I registered at the Merchant Pool Office and was immediately offered a job as a greaser on the Capetown Castle. This was the modern prestigious flagship of the Union Castle Line running a regular passenger and mail service to Capetown and Durban. I had never sailed on a passenger liner before and did not particularly want to. You did not get much time in port when you got there. You always knew where you were going, and it was not such an intimate life among such a large crew. However – there seemed to be nothing else available at the moment so I accepted a boarding pass to go aboard and see the Chief Engineer.

As I made my way through the docks I passed an ex Liberty ship in dry dock. I wondered whether it would be worth my while to board her and see if they had any vacancies. What a stroke of luck. They wanted a 5th. Engineer. After a long interview with the Chief and 2nd. Engineer they offered me the job. They were sailing tomorrow. The course of my life was to be settled for the next 5 years. How fate plays a part in ones life!

The Sedgepool was owned by Sir Robert Ropner & Co. Ltd., of West Hartlepool, well known and long established cargo fleet owners. She was originally built as a wartime Liberty ship in Savannah, Georgia, U.S.A. Like all the Liberty's built for Britain under Lend/Lease she had the prefix Sam to her name. She was called the Samdart. The 2nd.Mate, Bill Rush had been with her since her maiden voyage and liked to tell the story of how the original crew were sent to Savannah to collect her.

They were shipped out to New York on the Queen Mary and then trained down to Savannah expecting to go straight aboard her. On arrival at the shipyard the Captain went to the office to find out where she was berthed. The man in charge said "Samdart, Captain? Let me see now" as he thumbed through a pile of papers. "Ah, well now, the Samdart, she 'aint exactly ready for you yet Captain. Now why don't you and your crew go into town and enjoy some real old Georgia hospitality while we build her for you". "What do you mean, build her for us?" said the Captain. "I've just brought a whole crew over the Atlantic to collect her". "Well now, we sure as hell appreciate that Captain but I don't think we can have her ready for you in less than three weeks". The Captain nearly blew his top, but there was nothing he could do but accept the situation.

The crew were elated to have a nice break from the war and enjoy the tremendous hospitality of the good folks of Georgia. This was just as well as the crew had little money anyway!

The short end of the story is that the Samdart was built, had trials, loaded cargo and sailed in a record 18 days. Such was the ability and organisation of American Industry in the war years. The design of these prefabricated ships, which had been taken from a British design just before the war, was also excellent. They were flush decked with a cruiser stern. All the accommodation was 'amidships'. Officers and Petty Officers had their own cabins, and the crew all had two berth cabins. They carried about 10,000 tons of cargo and were good sea boats. There were instances where faulty welding caused some vessels to split in foul weather, and some sank. It was discovered that their hulls were prone to twisting in bad weather if ballast was carried in the 'tween decks. We were lucky. The Sedgepool stood up to all the sea could throw at her as we were to find out on more than one occasion.

As Fifth Engineer my duties were of a maintenance nature. I did not have to keep an engine room watch and worked day work. There was always enough to keep me going though. The worst job was cleaning the evaporator. The myriad salt encrusted tubes about 5/8" diameter needed constant cleaning. There were pumps and ancilliary equipment that needed overhaul from time to time. All deck equipment was my responsibility. I had to ensure that oil, grease etc. was kept up to scratch and machinery was in proper working order. It was a good job, allowing me to sleep well at nights and giving me plenty of time to study maintenance manuals etc.

We sailed the next day, straight out of dry dock where repairs to some under water fittings had been done as well as careening the bottom and painting with anti fouling paint. We were headed for Baltimore in Maryland U.S.A. in ballast. I still found it strange not to be sailing in convoy. The oceans of the world were a very vast and lonely place to be when nothing is in sight. There were of course many ships around within reasonable distance. Our radio operator thought it was like Piccadilly Circus as he twiddled his nobs and heard so much chatter going on.

Apart from a couple of the usual North Atlantic gales when we pitched and tossed for a few days, it was an uneventful voyage. We went straight to the coaling wharf when we arrived in Baltimore. Back to the old coal dust once again! We were to load 10,000 tons of the retched stuff for Birkenhead on the Mersey. Talk about taking coals to Newcastle!!!

The coaling wharf was a good way out of town and when I saw it I could see the reason why! We were told it would take no more than eight hours to load us and were warned that we would not have time to go into town before we sailed again. We were allowed ashore in the immediate vicinity though if we wanted a walk. It wasn't worth it. Coal dust lay everywhere.

It was fascinating to see them load us. Massive railway trucks, at last three times larger than ours in the U,K, were rolled down a long ramp at the end of which huge hydraulic clamps grabbed it on both sides as it went into a sort of loop like you had on roller coasters at a fairground. The whole truck emptied in to a large hopper in one go. Conveyor belts took the coal along to just above our cargo hold. A man sat in a rotating cab on the end of the conveyor belt and, as the coal shot off the end of it he swivelled it round so the coal was evenly distributed all over and even trimmed under the 'tween decks. No wonder they could load us so quickly! Mind you, the noise of these huge trucks being upended and cluttering back down the empty track was tremendous, the air was filled with coal dust. We had to batten everything down and shut ourselves in the saloon or our cabins as much as possible. We only spent 24 hours in Baltimore and were disappointed not to be able to see the City. However, we were certainly pleased to get away from that coaling wharf.

It was mid summer in the North Atlantic but we still managed to go through a couple of gales on the way home and there was always a heavy swell running between the gales. To me it was very pleasant. Having done a few crossings in mid winter in a tug, this was luxury sailing indeed! In fact I always used to get a bit bored in calm seas.

It took about a week to discharge our cargo in Birkenhead. We were to spend 10 days there altogether before sailing again and I took the opportunity to go home to Brighton for a week. Little did I know it would be nearly 5 years before I got home again!

We were to travel in ballast out to Vancouver for our next voyage. This was new ground for me. I looked forward to going through the Panama Canal and seeing the West coast of Canada for a change. As we headed south west the weather got warmer and in the Caribbean quite hot. As long as we met no Hurricanes all would be well.

We stopped at the Dutch West Indies Island of Curacao for bunkers, then went on to Colon at the eastern end of the Panama Canal where we dropped anchor to await our turn for passage through. The weather was very hot, humid and oppressive. The skies were invariably black and thunderstorms a daily occurence. The night sky would usually be lit up with tremendous lightning flashes from electrical storms.

The anchorage was full up with ships of all shapes, sizes and nationalities a bit reminiscent of wartime convoys. Passenger liners seemed to get priority to go through the canal. We were only held up overnight though and went through the next morning. It was a very efficiently run system. It had to be! There were quite a few locks to go through and ships passed in both directions and had to be lifted up and down to their various levels. Huge electrically driven 'Scammels' ran on rails alongside the locks. A stout wire was passed from them to the ship and we were dragged through the locks. Between each lock were large lakes with jungle down to the waters edge. It seemed a bit odd that wild jungle was so close to modern civilisation! I found the whole trip very interesting and looked forward to the return journey.

We left the Canal at Bilbao on the Pacific side and headed north for Vancouver. I think it took us about 8 days to get there. As we travelled past the Mexican and Californian coasts we encountered many porpoises, whales and seals. At one stage there were so many seals heads bobbing in the water they looked like hundreds of footballs.

H.M.S. Trafalgar entering the Gatun Lock,, the first on the Caribbean side. The three step lock takes a ship up 84 feet above sea level.

A modern container ship in the Miroflores Lock.

It was October 1947 when we entered the forest laden coast of British Columbia and steamed into Vancouver. A distinct chill was in the air, but the most magnificent scenery all around. We were to load grain in the bottom of the ship and sawn timber on top including a high deck cargo. Before loading the grain the ship had to be sealed and fumigated so we were all put ashore in a hotel for three days while this was done.

We all enjoyed Vancouver and the many interesting places to visit. One thing that amused me were the bars. Unlike the east coast where there were no bars, in Vancouver there were separate ones for men and women. Signs outside would say ‘Men’ or ‘Women’. I thought they were public toilets at first!

Once the fumigating had been done we moved to the large grain silo’s at the North end of the harbour and took on that part of our cargo. This filled our holds about a quarter full. We then went under the Lion Gate Bridge (a bit like the Golden Gate in San Francisco) to New Westminster where we loaded a part cargo of timber.

Our next move was to Vancouver Island where we loaded more timber at various small ports around the coast. I say ‘ports’ lightly as some places were no more than saw mills with a wooden jetty running out to sea for ships to tie up to. Canadian Indians loaded us up.

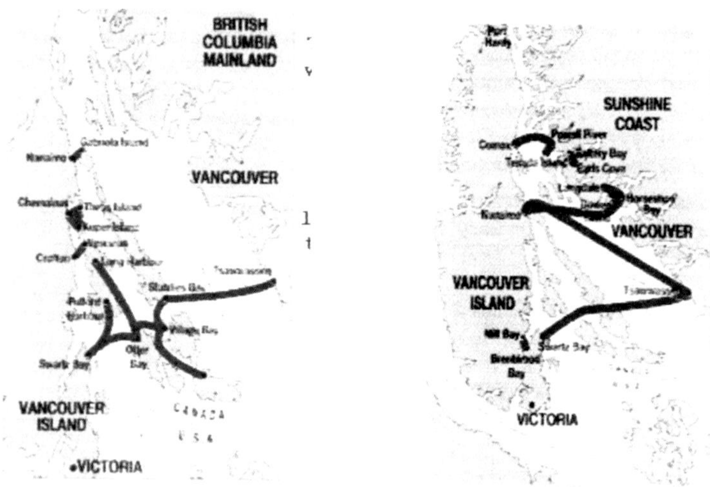

The waters around Vancouver Sound were very treacherous.

I was hoping we would go to the Islands capital, Victoria but there was no indication that we would. I had known a girl in Brighton who had married the Adjutant to the Victoria Scottish Regiment, a Captain Parks, and they were living there. We were loading in Croften, about 50 miles from Victoria and, as there was nothing for me to do on board I took the day off and hitch hiked to Victoria. Most of the few cars seen on that road were ancient Model 'A' or 'T' Fords. I had no trouble hitching a lift though .No one passed anyone by in that sort of country in those days. I found the Parks in the phone book and was immediately asked round for a drink and a chat. They had a large house, built like most with overlapped timber but extremely warm and comfortable. It was the first time I had seen a typical Canadian construction whereby the whole of the basement of the house was one large room. Down here was the boiler, Deep Freeze, Washing Machine, work bench and tools, plenty of storage space for logs burnt on the open fire in the lounge upstairs and finally double remote controlled doors so cars could be driven in under the house. The most practical way of building a house I ever saw. I vowed that I would build a similar house in England if ever I got the chance. Everything was so easily accessible and left the upstairs living quarters free of any encumbrance.

Dorothy was very pleased to see me and chat about old times and old friends. 'Parky' also made me very welcome. They insisted that, as it was such a long way back I should stay the night and have a meal with them. I would find it much more difficult to hitch a ride back to Croften. It was not the sort of place many people went to. I was more than pleased to accept their invitation.

Perhaps I should mention that the reason I hitched a lift rather than get the once a day bus was that, due to the exchange rate regulations in force in the U.K. at that time we were only allowed to draw $10 a week of our pay while in Canada or the U.S. This was pretty well useless. It was like having a £1 note in your pocket in England and expecting it to last a week while you were on holiday. Even U.K. tourists travelling anywhere in the world were only allowed to take £25 out of the country and this was stamped in your passport.

I enjoyed a good meal and wine with the Parks during which 'Parky' said "What a pity you will not be here next week, it is the annual Regimental Ball at the Armoury and you could have come as our guest". However, I knew I would not be able to make it so that was that.

The next morning 'Parky' insisted on giving me my bus fare back to Croften so, although feeling a bit embarrassed, I was very pleased to accept his offer. As I guessed I would have some difficulty in hitching back.

I arrived back on board to find our holds now full of timber and we sailed yet again to a somewhat larger town called Nanaimo. Here we were to load our deck cargo. While here we witnessed demonstrations by the Dukhabors. These people were of early Russian descent whose forebears had crossed the Bering Strait into Alaska many years ago and found there way down here to settle. I do not know what their 'beef' was, but they caused any amount of trouble with their demonstrations in this part of the world. We saw them marching stark naked through the town, and this was in November! The Mounties had a big job rounding them up.

Our deck cargo was loaded to Bridge height. We looked top heavy but of course were not. Catwalks were made for the crew to walk along just like we had on the old ss Veni when we carried timber.

We sailed for home on December 3rd 1947. The Pilot came aboard at dusk and off we went, disappointed that we would be somewhere in the Atlantic and at sea for Christmas.

It was a dark evening and drizzling with rain as we left Nanaimo. I was down in the engine room for some reason or other when, about an hour after we sailed there was a sudden grinding crash. The ship heeled over to port and shuddered to a stop. I was nearly thrown in among the huge pistons. I just managed to grab a guardrail as I slid across the engine room plates. The Pilot had put us ashore. I went up on deck to see what had happened. There was no danger of us sinking with all this timber aboard. Thee was a lot of running about by the deck crew and shouting of orders which could hardly be heard above the noise of the of steam blowing off from the boilers safety valve now the engine was stopped.

We soon found we were taking water in the bilges and all pumps were immediately put to work. Grain could be seen floating out of the ship so we knew we had been holed.

We had gone aground on a high tide so there was some concern about what might happen as the tide dropped. It did drop by 11 feet and we took a 15 degree list to port as well as dropping by the stern but we seemed to be holding there alright.

We notified the Authorities of our predicament and a few hours later a salvage expert came out in a motor launch. He surveyed our situation and sent for his company's large salvage tug the 'Salvage Chieftain'. It arrived the next morning but in spite of some long and hefty pulling it failed to get us off the rocks. The next day another tug the 'Island Warrior' came to give them some help. The two of them had to wait for the next highest tide and even then had a hard job pulling us off. Once they succeeded the ship settled down to an even keel but was well down by the head. However- we were able to steam the 40 miles to Victoria under our own steam.

We had been aground for three days and all the local radio reports kept putting out bulletins on our situation. The newspapers were also full of our misfortune so when we finally docked in 'Victoria' the first of many people I saw on the quayside was Dorothy and Parky. News of our imminent arrival had been broadcast and they had come down especially to see if I could go to their Regimental Ball after all ? It was to be held the next day. I O.K.'d it with the Chief Engineer and they said they would pick me up the next day.

ss. 'Sedgepool'
on Provost Point, Vancouver Island with 'Salvage Chieftain' in attendance.

Perhaps the Pilot could not see the sign in the dark !

Another view of our grounding. All pictures from the 'Daily Colonist', 'Victoria' December 4th 1947

Alongside at Victoria. Half the deck cargo already unloaded but still down by the head a bit.

The first thing that had to be done was to unload the complete cargo. We would then go into the large Dry Dock at the nearby Naval Base at Esquimault. We knew then that we would definitely be here for Christmas. In fact it was over two months before we finally got repaired, reloaded and sailed again. I looked forward to a lengthy stay in this beautiful part of the world, particularly as I had some good friends ashore.

Our main problem was that we could only draw $10 a week from our pay! A few of the crew managed to get part time jobs ashore in the evenings and at weekends. But for most life became very boring after a while.

I decided that I could do with a radio in my cabin to listen to while on board. I saw one advertised in the local paper for $10. A weeks allowance! But I still thought it worthwhile. I went round to the address given, a flat in a three story house. A youngish man opened the door. I said I had come about the radio? He bid me enter and showed me a small mantle type radio in a bakelite case. It worked alright so I thought this will do! He then said "You are English , aren't you?" To which I replied "Yes". "Would you like a beer?" I was asked. Who was I to refuse a free beer! He and his young wife seemed eager to hear how things were in England these days, and when I told them I was from the Sedgepool another can of beer was immediately offered. When I finally left their flat that night, having helped to consume a whole case of beer, they insisted I take the radio for nothing. How lucky can you get?

The Empress Hotel in Victoria. At night its outline is lit up by thousands of bulbs making it look like a crystal palace.

Anyway, I am getting a bit ahead of myself. Getting back to the Regimental Ball, 'Parky' picked me up the day after we arrived in Victoria. He came soon after lunch, saying "We thought you might as well come and have a quiet afternoon with us and have some tea before the start of the pretty hectic night that was ahead of us!"

It was a 'Dress' affair of course, so I wore my best uniform. (My only one). My wartime medals were at home with Mother but I had the ribbons sewn on to my jacket. I felt a bit 'overdressed' as Parky picked me up as he was in casuals. The situation was soon reversed later in the afternoon when they both disappeared to get changed, leaving me with a couple of drinks.

Dorothy was the first to emerge, dressed in a beautiful blue evening dress with gold trimmings. Parky fair drew my breath away when he appeared in full Highland Dress with Kilt, Scarlet Tunic, Medals, Adjutants Sash, White Spats, Dirk in his sock and Busby under his arm. He looked magnificent. We had a last 'Wee Dram' while waiting for the Taxi they had ordered. No way was Parky driving tonight! We eventually pulled up outside the Victorian Scottish Regiments H.Q. known as 'The Armoury'. It was a magnificent edifice built like an old Scottish Castle. The large grey granite stones of the building were castellated around the top. Round towers were incorporated in the corners. The whole was surrounded by a dry moat and entrance was over a draw bridge and through a huge overhead trellis gate with spiked bottoms.

There were many cars and taxis discharging their very colourful occupants when we arrived. Other ranks, also in full highland dress, checked everyone in past the guardhouse into the magnificent flagstone covered courtyard. The roof was supported by large granite pillars each one of which had a flaming firebrand burning in an iron basket about 6 feet off the ground. Rows of white sheeted tables were laid out for dinner. The Officers table at the top end sported an excellent array of the Regimental Silver. The whole scene was breathtaking. I remarked that MGM could not have done better in a film set.

I was ushered in to the Officers Mess which had a long bar along one wall. I was introduced to the Colonel and many other officers. I said " I feel a bit like a blackhead on a film stars face among such finery in my Navy Blue uniform!" but I was made very welcome. 'Parky' introduced me as an old friend of Dorothy's in dock on the Sedgepool. They had all heard of our mishap and wanted to know about it first hand so I found myself busily engaged repeating our story to many. The Colonel approved my being made an Honorary Member of the Mess during my stay in Victoria. However – I knew I would not be able to avail myself of this on my meagre $10 a week.

We were chatting away at the bar when suddenly the shrill blast of a bugle deafened all conversation. It was the call to dinner. Once everyone was in their places the sound of the bagpipes echoed throughout as the Colonel and his Lady were led to their places by the Regimental Piper. Slow handclaps from the whole assembly accompanied their march. Grace was said by the Padre and we all sat down to a very memorable meal. Outside caterers had prepared the meal and were serving it so all ranks could enjoy this memorable occasion together. I was sitting at the top table alongside ' 'Parky' and Dorothy, about 6 places away from the Colonel. I really did feel out of place in my blue uniform and apologised again for spoiling the picture, but was to worry about it.

After dinner we all retired to the bar again while the tables were cleared away for dancing. At onstage the conversation got round to sport and it appeared that the Regiment had a Rugby fixture against a team of Fiji Islanders who were over here to collect a recently built ship. Rugby was in its infancy in British Columbia at the time but was becoming very popular. Apparently the Regiment was having a job to get an experienced team together and I, rather foolishly, and no doubt talking through my drinks, mentioned that I used to play regularly before the war. I was immediately pounced upon to play for the Regiment and again, what with the drinks, felt I ought to do something to repay my hosts for such a magnificent evening. I found myself agreeing to play for them. I had not played since before the war when I was a very fast wing three quarter, but this was boys Rugby, not mans. I was also now completely out of training. I think the Regiment expected great things of me but I was probably the worst man on the field. The Fiji's played in their bare feet, as was their custom, and we were all a bit afraid of treading on them. They also had some very large men in their side who were difficult to bring down in a tackle. All in all we found ourselves completely outplayed as a team. Anyway, it was only a friendly game and no one seemed to be embarrassed by the fact that we were truly trounced. It was a good experience for the Regiment. I was totally stiff in all joints and muscles for about two weeks afterwards. "Never again" I thought!

Getting back to the Armoury. It was announced that the floor was ready for dancing, and the versatile Regimental Band, playing a variety of instruments, gave an excellent performance. An interval had been arranged half way through the evening and during this time the Regimental Pipers and Drummers gave a spectacular demonstration of marching and counter marching as they played. In front of the Band a trooper led the Regimental Mascot, a huge St. Bernard dog. The whole scene had to be seen to be believed. Edinburgh would have been very proud of its compatriots. A demonstration of Scottish Dancing followed the bands display before dancing continued until the early hours of the morning. The whole evening had been a tremendous success and would be a night I would be privileged to remember for the rest of my life.

The night of the Ball was December 6th. 1947. Life continued apace on board the ship. We took the opportunity while in Dry Dock to do our own Boiler Clean and other minor repairs and overhauls of pumps, bearings and equipment. That kept us occupied until Christmas.

The most unusual thing about Christmas Day was that I ate three Christmas Dinners. Although I knew I was going to 'Parky' for dinner at 3 p.m. I felt I would be conspicuous by my absence if I did not join my fellow officers for dinner on board at 12 noon. I was feeling 'very replete' therefore when I arrived at 'Parkys' but never the less managed to do justice to the excellent meal they served. We all managed to have a sleep in the armchair afterwards which was very fortunate as we were going out to 'Parky's' for yet another dinner in the evening. This turned out to be a large family gathering and included a wonderful 95 year old character in Captain Grey, a one time Captain of the Cutty Sark. I had some great conversations with him and we were to meet up again 2 or 3 times during my stay in Victoria.

I was introduced to one of the Captains Granddaughters named Eileen Grey. She was the advertising Editor of the Daily Colonist newspaper. She seemed very interested to hear of my worldly travels and wartime experiences. We arranged to meet again during my stay in Victoria. Eileen was a little older than me and a divorcee. She had an 8 year old daughter who suffered from T.B. She was in a Solarium up on the beautiful Malahat Drive a few miles out of town. I went with her a couple of times to visit her daughter.

The Doctors told Eileen that it might do her daughter some good if she were to travel south through different climatic changes, taking it slowly. She had made plans therefore to drive right down the west coast of America and across the bottom to New Orleans, looking for stories for her newspaper on the way to help pay for the trip. I told her how envious I was. I would love to have done such a trip. She obviously gave some thought to what I had said, because one day she asked me if I would like to join her. She said "I could use some help and company and you would be some protection for us". I jumped at the chance, but it was not to be. No way would the Captain let me leave the ship. I had signed articles that I would remain with her until we returned to a U.K. port. I was adamant that I would leave somehow. He said he would have me arrested if I 'Jumped ship'. I tried to plead sickness to get ashore, but to no avail. Eileen had to leave without me. I often wonder where life would have taken me had I been allowed to go along with her. Such is fate!

We were well into January 1948 by now and it looked as though it would be about another month before we would be ready to sail for home again. Most of the crew were getting a bit bored as, in spite of the beauty of our surroundings, there was little we could do on $10 a week. The Labour Government came in for a 'lot of stick' for continuing to keep us in this predicament.

However – the day finally came when the Dry Dock was flooded. We went alongside the quay where our cargo was re-loaded. I said my fond farewells to 'Parky' and Dorothy and all their friends who threw a farewell party for me. Although looking forward to going home, I had a distinct feeling of wanting to stay in this beautiful country.

We eventually sailed for home about the third week in February. (I think we had a different Pilot aboard this time !!!) The run down the west coast of America was calm, warm and interesting. There were many ships sailing up and down the coast and others crossing our bows as they headed in from across the Pacific to the many American ports down that coast. The large shoals of seals were still bobbing about like footballs on the surface of the sea. Sharks, whales and dolphins were plentiful as we headed further south

My little radio would pick up different local stations as we passed various towns and cities but I found it 'gave up, the ghost' as we got past Los Angeles. No doubt we were out of range of any stations as we passed the barren lands of Baja California and the Mexican coast.

The deck officers were kept very busy as we entered the Gulf of Panama. Apart from some islands in the middle of the gulf, shipping was extremely busy with ships heading in all directions as they left or were heading for the Canal. Plenty of trawlers and inshore fishing boats added to the hazards and when visibility dropped to almost zero during the frequent tropical downpours, the deck watch had to be particularly alert.

Once again the Panama Canal held its fascination as we fortunately passed through in daylight. Once through we headed for Curacao again to top up with bunkers. From then on it was an uneventful trip home across the

Atlantic. As is usual on all merchant ships heading home the crew speculated on where we would discharge our cargo. We found ourselves entering the River Mersey once again but this time we did not stop. We picked up a Pilot who took us up through the Manchester ship canal and eventually tied up at Salford docks, a very run down and depressing area of Manchester at that time. I believe it has altered a lot for the better now.

I had been aboard the Sedgepool about 6 months by now and thought I would take an extended leave and have a change of ship. However – the Chief told me that our next trip was a 6 month round the world voyage. We were going out through the Suez Canal to Japan, then across the Pacific to Vancouver again and home through the Panama. This was very tempting! I had never been to Japan before and might not get another chance! I decided to remain with her then and meanwhile went down to Brighton for 10 days leave while the ship discharged her cargo.

There was little to interest me in Brighton in those days. I had no real friends and Mother was working most of the time. I spent hours in the 'Bullfrogs Club' in North St. This was an old haunt of Dorothy from Victoria and I was able to appraise all her old friends of her new lifestyle over there.

I was really quite pleased when my leave was over, and even more pleased to leave Salford and its grimy surroundings. We went down to Cardiff and, guess what? We loaded coal again for Port Said in Egypt. Back to the old coal dust everywhere again! There were still a large number of coal burning ships traversing the world in those days and the British Merchant Navy, as before the war, was lucratively engaged in depositing bunker coal at many points around the world for these ships to obtain their coal supplies. I have no doubt that many a stoker was more than pleased to be getting the best Welsh Steam Coal in a place like Port Said!

Our 5-6 week stay there was pretty miserable! There were no grab cranes on the quayside and the method of discharging the cargo was to have rows of planks strung out along the length of the ship in the form of steps. In the hold would be labourers shovelling the coal into large baskets which would be lifted out by our derricks. This meant we had to keep steam up all the time to work the winches. The baskets would then be carried down the stepped planks by more labourers who would then tip them into carts pulled by Mules or Donkeys. These labourers swarmed all over the place like an army of ants. The work for them was horrendous in the heat of Port Said. The Mediterranean is non tidal so, as the ship rose higher in the water even more planks had to be added for them to climb. The heat and coal dust everywhere were as much as we could tolerate so goodness knows what these poor retches felt doing this ' slave labour' job for a mere pittance of a wage!

Once the coal was discharged the ship was washed down, the holds washed out with high pressure hoses and allowed to dry in the sun. We then loaded 10,000 tons of salt for Japan. At least the method of loading was a bit different. The planks were removed form the side of the ship, the salt was brought in by the same Mule or Donkey carts and dumped on the quayside. Labourers then shovelled it in to steel buckets which were winched aboard by our derricks. A line was attached to the bottom of the buckets which, when pulled by a man standing at the top of the hold, tipped the salt out of the bucket. All five holds were worked at the same time and it was amazing how quickly we got fully laden.

Once loaded the hatches were battened down and we were more than pleased to get away from Port Said! We sailed on down through the canal and the Red Sea, where my mind brought back memories of my last trip towing a floating dock on the Naval Tug H.M.R.T. 'Assiduous' with stops at Port Sudan and Massawa on the way. We stopped at Aden for bunkers. Bunkering was done by means of an oil pipeline run out along the sea bed to a buoy floating in the middle of the harbour. We tied up to two other buoys fore and aft and connected our hose up. It only took a couple of hours to fill our tanks so there was no time to go ashore. Not that I wanted to! I had spent more than enough time here on the 'Assiduous'. The extreme heat that reflected off the barren, rocky hills around Aden's Harbour was more than anyone wanted to relish for long. I noted the dry dock we towed there 4 years ago was still in use.

One incident that occurred on this occasion sticks well in my memory! The weather had been so hot that many of us slept on deck at night. As we only had a short stay for bunkers and were not tied up alongside I had not bothered to take my bedding back into my cabin. We were having lunch when someone came in and asked who had left their bedding on deck. It was me of course. I was told it was now drying off on the harbour wall. Local thieves had waited until there was no boat alongside to give chase and every one would be at lunch. They then rowed out in a small dinghy, climbed up the mooring ropes and stole whatever they could. I shouted at them but they only waved back, laughing. I lost all my bedding and was duly charged by the company for its replacement.

Aden was our last port of call before reaching Yokohama. It took us about 5 weeks to get there. Down the Indian Ocean, round Ceylon (Sri Lanka) across the Bay of Bengal, through the Malacca Straits to Singapore then Borneo and the South China Sea. Up to now we had a pretty boring journey. The seas had been mostly flat and calm with an oily appearance on the surface. The heat was oppressive. The electrical storms every night were quite magnificent to watch as the whole sky was continually lit up with tremendous flashes of lightning.

We were soon into the South China Sea and it was the Typhoon Season. We had warning over the radio as to what to expect and we were not disappointed! The sky blackened in the middle of the day. The wind rose to a crescendo from nowhere. It was soon impossible to go on deck with any degree of safety. Huge waves engulfed the whole ship as she rolled violently. This was far worse than the North Atlantic Hurricanes I had experienced. It was really quite frightening! The scream of the wind, the crash of the waves as they pounded the ship and made her shudder drowned all other sounds. The only good thing about the Typhoon was that it passed us by in 24 hours. Unlike the Atlantic Hurricanes that often lasted for days. We were certainly glad to see the back of this Typhoon and thankful the ship had stood up to it so well. It was not uncommon for ships to founder in these waters, and I think it might have been in this Typhoon that one of our Naval tugs H.M.R.T. 'Enticer' foundered and was lost with all hands! We knew that from then on the Sedgepool was capable of taking anything the seas could throw at her and were comforted by the thought!

We eventually arrived in Yokohama in Tokyo Bay just a few miles from Tokyo itself. We anchored out in the large Bay which was extremely busy with much shipping. There was no room for us alongside a wharf so we had to discharge our cargo the hard way again. Large Sampans came alongside us. Labourers went down into the holds and shovelled the salt into large steel buckets once more. These were hauled up by our own derricks and swung over the side to be tipped into the Sampans which, when fully loaded disappeared under their own power to 'Lord knows where'. It was shocking work for the labourers who worked a very long day in the most arduous of conditions.

Each Sampan was owned by the family who lived aboard it. The wife could be seen cooking, washing and looking after the children in the small quarters they had on the stern of the vessel. They all looked extremely poor people to me, in spite of owning their own boat. It was a way of life passed on by their forebears.

We were all keen to get ashore after six weeks at sea and see what Japan was like. The first blow came when we were told there was no facility for us to draw any pay here, but the resourceful sailor could always find 'ways and means'!

Before we left England I had spoken to other seamen who had been to Japan and was told there was no sugar out there. Saccharin Tablets were therefore a very good source of money making. I had stocked up with about 100,000 of these tiny tablets only to find on arrival that the Americans had started shipping sugar in and I had quite a job selling them for what I paid. The best barter was cigarettes and Lux toilet soap. A small sixpenny tablet of Lux fetched 200 yen about 10/- at that time. I forget what we got for cigarettes but it was a very handsome profit. I managed to stuff 2,000 about my person in flat tins of 50 State Express brand. I wore my loose fitting Burberry raincoat so the bulges would not be too obvious.

Armed American Army Police (called Snowdrops because of their distinctive white helmets) were posted at the dock gates as we went ashore. We were nearly always searched but on this occasion I got away with it. I soon sold the cigarettes and even finished up selling my Burberry for a jolly good price. The shops were full of very interesting things. You would never have thought they had just lost a war! The main purchase I remember making was of a tiny 35mm Camera that would fit into a matchbox. It was solidly made of stainless steel and must have been one of your typical spy cameras. It took excellent pictures and some time later I sold it for a handsome profit in Australia.

The pity of it was there was little we could do in Japan at this time. The country was under very strict American rule. We were not allowed to travel anywhere. Not even to Tokyo. In any event, as we could draw no pay and the clamp down on Black Market trading was ruthlessly observed by the U.S.Army police. It was too risky to take the chance of getting stopped and asked where you got your money from!

I was lucky to get ashore with my first lot of contraband. After that we were all thoroughly searched whenever we went ashore. We did not think much of the strict rigidity to rule exercised by the Snowdrops. After all, we had just spent 6 weeks at sea and would be spending even longer when we left. You would have thought they could have given us some latitude! But it was not to be and we were glad when we eventually sailed again. Japan is a very beautiful country and I was only sorry that, having travelled so far I was unable to see any of it!

Then came a big shock to us all. We were not going back to Vancouver and home through the Panama Canal. The ship had been chartered to carry Phosphate Fertilizer from the tiny Island of Nauru on the equator, to Australia and New Zealand.

Nauru was a typical volcanic eruption that had occurred many thousands of years ago and was now dormant. Generations of sea birds had nested there and deposited large quantities of Guano, now very valuable as a fertilizer to countries like Australia and New Zealand. The island was only 12 miles in circumference and about 360 miles from the next nearest island. It was very flat and drew on the skills of our Navigating officers to find it at all. As it was right on the equator itself I suppose theoretically, once you had found your latitude all you had to do was sail along it until you came across the island!
Sales of the Guano deposit had made the small population of the island the richest per capita people in the world and when we arrived we could see why? Numerous ships similar to ours were drifting off the island waiting their turn to load. There was no harbour here but a large steel framework had been built out over the Coral Reef which carried the conveyor belt loading the ships. We could only load when the sea was flat calm as we had to tie up to two buoys fore and aft over the reef and try to keep the ship steady under the conveyor while loading. We were right on the edge of the reef with a sheer drop below us. Loading took about 8 hours.

NAURU showing the Phosphate quarry in the middle of the island, and the Coral Reef surrounding it from which there was a sheer drop of thousands of feet.
(Photograph taken by a Liberator bomber during the war and before the loading elevator was built. National Geographic Magazine)

A small motor boat came out from the shore. It was explained to us that we would have to drift off the island for about two weeks waiting our turn to load. The sea was oily calm with no breeze at all and we were right on the equator so it was very hot. We soon became bored and fed up with nothing to do. The first few days were spent shark fishing. There were plenty of them around, no doubt attracted by the 'gash' the cooks were throwing overboard from so many ships. At least they kept the surface of the sea clean from floating garbage! We could not of course, go in for a swim as we would dearly loved to have done!

To catch the sharks, we used a meat hook from the galley on the end of a ½" thick rope. A bit of old meat on the hook, dangle it on the surface and a shark was caught as quick as a flash. We got quite excited when we caught our first one, but found it very difficult to kill. There skins were as tough as steel. The skipper came down with a .38 revolver. The first bullet just bounced off the sharks skin. It took one through the eye to kill it.
Various schemes were thought up by those wanting to relieve their boredom. They would catch two sharks and tie their tails together then throw them back in the sea again. They then watched the powerful struggle for life as they fought to get away from each other. A shark must swim

Quarrying the Guano deposits. It seems hard to believe that all this is bird droppings!

forward and let the water pass through its gills if it is to stay alive. Others were tied to empty oil drums which were watched until they disappeared over the horizon. At one time we had thirty sharks hanging around the stern of the ship and smelling to high heaven. Can you be cruel to a shark?

We were more than pleased when it became our turn to go in and load our cargo. There were no tugs and it required a lot of skill to get under the conveyor and tie up to the two buoys. Two motor boats came out and took our lines which they then reeved through shackles on the buoys. If a breeze came up and we had to leave in a hurry, we could slip the wires ourselves and steam off.

Loading the crushed Phosphate under the elevator. The whole ship getting covered in thick dust during the process.

Map of Polynesia.

HOBART seen from Mount Wellington over 4,000 feet high and snow capped much of the year.

Once in position no time was lost in starting to load. Our 10,000 tons were loaded in eight hours but we had to suffer a ship covered in fine phosphate dust. It was worse than coal dust. All portholes and doors had to be kept shut so it got 'pretty warm' inside the ship! We were well pleased to get away from that Coral Reef and get the ship hosed down and under way again. Our destination was Hobart, the capital of Tasmania and it took us two weeks to get there.

By the time we arrived in Hobart it had been seven weeks since we had set foot ashore in Yokohama and six weeks before that since we were in Port Said. Everyone was itching to get ashore in a cool, English speaking country again. We had 2-3 months pay we could draw on so anticipated having a 'drink or two'!

The entrance to Hobart reminded me of St. Johns, Newfoundland. We sailed by very high cliffs along the coastline before coming to an entrance which opened up into one of the largest deep water harbours in the world. The City lay on a narrow strip of flat plain at the foot of the over 4,000 foot high Mount Wellington.

I do not remember much about the place now only that, as was usual with most sailors after a long spell at sea, you headed for the nearest café for a shore cooked meal and then found a suitable bar for the rest of the evening.

We spent 10 days in Hobart unloading our cargo, replenishing ships stores, watering and bunkering before we returned to Nauru for another load. This was certainly a very lucrative trade for the ships owners.

On arrival at Nauru life became very boring again while we waited our turn to load. Once loaded we headed south once more but this time went to Melbourne to discharge. This sounded like a much more promising and interesting place to go! The voyage down was uneventful the weather being fine and warm with calm seas. The deck officers had plenty to keep them alert and interested as they navigated us down through the Solomon Islands, Guadalcanal and the Coral sea. Many other small islands dotted the ocean as we sailed down past the Great Barrier Reef. As we got further south and past Sydney in New South Wales, we at last got a freshening and cooler breeze. The seas got a bit rougher as we turned into the Bass Strait between Tasmania and Victoria where some movement was quite perceptible. There was always at least a heavy swell in the Bass Strait as the uninterrupted winds blew right across the Indian Ocean from South Africa. The Great

Australian Bight can be very rough indeed and in fact usually is. Many of the old sailing ships had been wrecked along these dangerous shores.

We picked up a Pilot at the entrance to Port Phillip Bay and he took us up to the top end of the Bay where we entered the River Yarra and finally found our berth in Melbourne itself.

Melbourne is a great City. Its suburbs stretch for miles and many have British names like Brighton and St. Kilda. There was plenty to interest us ashore. Good shops and large department stores. Cinemas, Theatres, and of course, 'Pubs'. The only thing was that women did not go into the pubs, and opening hours were from 10 a.m. until 6 p.m.

From 5-6 p.m. was known as 'the 5 o'clock swill'. This is when the workers knocked off work at 5 p.m. and made a dash for the nearest pub and downed as many drinks as they could in the hour on their way home. The Bartenders would have the whole bar covered ready with full glasses of ice cold beer in time for the rush. I found the beer to be quite strong and too many left you with one devil of a headache the next day!

The Australian penchant for gambling was much in evidence wherever you went. Even on the docks, as soon as you stepped ashore you would find the Dockers playing their national game of 'Two up' known as Zwei. It entailed one man putting whatever money he wanted to in the 'kitty'. Then all the others would bet whatever amount they wanted from that kitty on the way two pennies fell which the kitty holder tossed into the air. Two heads, two tails or odds. I have seen as much as £2,000 being gambled on the floor, and that was in 1949.

There were two excellent race courses in Melbourne, Caulfield and Moonee Valley. Some of us went to Moonee Valley on Saturday afternoon. We had an excellent lunch in the Restaurant and managed quite a few beers while watching the afternoon racing. We all had 'beginners luck'. Two horse in different races were named Britisher and Londoner. We just HAD to back those. We did and they both won at long odds.

When racing was over we were 'in the money' so went to a high class restaurant where we had Sydney Bay Oysters on ice, a large Rump Steak and a 'bottle or two' of good Red Australian wine.

After our meal we went to Caulfield racecourse where they had 'Trotting races' in the evening. This entailed a horse pulling a very light cart called a 'sulky' with the jockey sitting on a very small seat aboard the sulky.

Harness straps along the length of the horse were designed to keep the animal at a 'trotting' pace. If the horse broke this pace it was disqualified and you lost your money. It was all very interesting and exciting but, needless to say, our winnings from the afternoon were lost in the evening. Anyway, we had a jolly good day out and paid all our expenses from what we had won.

We were about 10 days in Melbourne before sailing for Nauru yet again. We had now been away from home about 6 months and realised that, had our original plan been kept to we should have arriving home about now. How much longer we would be kept on this run to Nauru we had no idea but we were getting a bit tired of it. There was nothing we do about it though. When you signed on a ship at home you signed that you would remain with her until she arrived back at a U.K. port, whether that be 2 weeks or two years or more. These days crews are flown home on regular leaves or replacement from all over the world, and many officers take their wives on trips with them.

CHAPTER ELEVEN

GEELONG, VICTORIA, AUSTRALIA

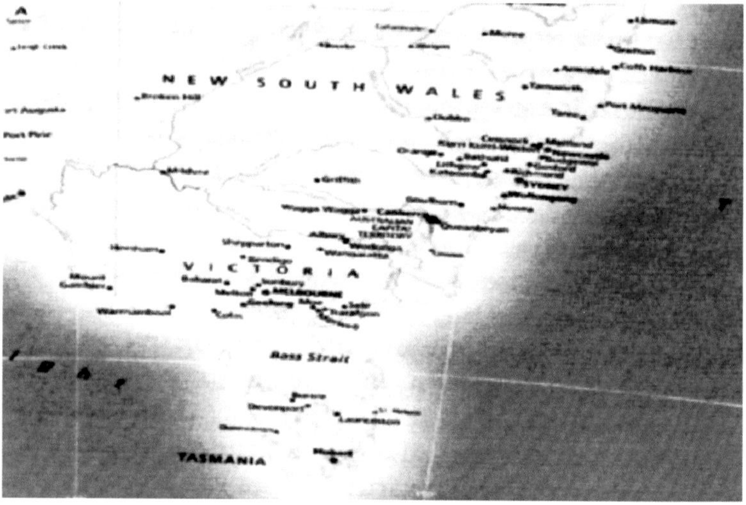

We did our third trip to Nauru and came back to Port Phillip Bay to discharge our cargo at Geelong just inside the entrance to the bay and 50 miles from Melbourne. Geelong is a beautiful place, well known for its wool industry. The old four masted sailing clippers used to have a regular run here to collect the wool cargoes for the U.K.

It was a Saturday morning when we tied up to the long wooden jetty that jutted out into the circular harbour. We had the weekend off and a few of us (sixteen in fact) decided to join forces and go ashore for a drink about 11 a.m. As was usual when we did this, one man was appointed treasurer and we all chipped in 10/- each to start with. He then paid for all drinks, food, taxis or whatever we needed to spend money on. If that ran out we all put more into the kitty. It worked out very well and ensured we never had to bother about whose round it was next!

We found a sizeable bar called the 'Prince of Wales' just off the main street. No singing was allowed in Australian bars in those days, but we discovered they had a separate room with a piano in it. Our Carpenter was an excellent piano player, and we asked the Landlord if we could use this room and have a sing song. He said we were welcome. No doubt 16 thirsty sailors could have anything they wanted in his eyes!

It was not long before we had a good sing song going, and a bit later a couple of Australians poked their head round the door and asked if they could join us? We told them they were welcome as long as they put there 10/- in the kitty!

A little while later one of them (a little bit worse for drink) said something insulting to the youngest member of our party. He nonchalantly dismissed the remark with a "Why don't you go home", upon which the Aussie attacked him. I stepped in to come to his assistance and separate them. 'Chippy' stopped playing the piano and the singing stopped. The Landlord came in to see what was going on and told the Aussies to leave.

A little while later another Aussie poked his head round the door and said " The Footscray football club from Melbourne are waiting outside for you lot". The two earlier miscreants apparently belonged to that club who were on a days outing and spoiling for the opportunity of a fight. We wanted no trouble and a couple of us went outside to try and calm down the situation. There was no one there. They thought we would be too scared to go out the front way and would try and doge out the back and that is where they were waiting. We all went out to try and placate them but taunts were thrown at us and fists started flying. They were a fit team of strong young men, but had obviously had a lot more drink than we had and, surprisingly, were no match for the crew of the Sedgepool. We gave an extremely good account of ourselves before the police arrived and broke the fight up. The Landlord told the police that WE were quite harmless and the Footscray crowd had just been looking for trouble. The police ran them out of town. As I was the only officer among us, the Police Chief invited me back to his office to help him make out a report on the situation. During this time he produced a bottle of Rum from his desk drawer and together we made quite an inroad into it. He told me this football team had a bad reputation for causing trouble wherever they went and he was more than pleased at the beating we had given them. I said I was amazed at our performance myself. We had all been together a very long time and never had one man as much as step out of line before. We were NOT a belligerent crowd.

The next day, Sunday, I suddenly had a recurrence of the external hemorrhoid troubles I had in Massawa some two years ago aboard the 'Assiduous'. It got so bad and painful that by Monday I could hardly walk. I told the skipper I would have to see a Doctor. One was sent for. He immediately said I had no choice but to go straight into hospital for an operation. This would mean a three week stay in hospital and time for recuperation afterwards. I was crestfallen. I would have to leave the ship. I packed my gear and waited for an Ambulance to collect me.

I was taken to the Geelong Cottage Hospital and the first man I saw in bed was one of the Footscray football team. His face was black, blue and yellow all over and he was in a right old mess. Thus was my introduction to Geelong!

In spite of the fact this was a 'Cottage Hospital', the men's ward contained 30 beds, fifteen down each side. The chap in the next bed to me was in for the same operation. He was Len McKiernan, an ex soldier who had been in the siege of Tobruk in the North African desert. Len was a great character and we soon became very friendly. He had so many people in to see him every day that one day he 'blew his top' and said " Christ almighty mates, why don't you go and talk to 'Lofty' in the next bed so I can have a word with my wife". In the end they started coming in to see me. They brought no end of baked custards and the like for me to eat.

The Eastern Beach, Geelong. The swimming area , surrounded by a shark protection solid fence, can be seen behind the three Palm Trees.

We had a Ward Sister called Cassidy of ex Irish stock. We called her 'Whirlwind Cassidy'. She would wake us all up at the unearthly hour of 3a.m. and dash round the ward sticking a thermometer in everyone's mouth. Half an hour later she would come round and collect them. Then thirty bowls of lukewarm water would be distributed for us all to wash and shave. Beds would be made and tidied up so all was 'shipshape' before 6 a.m. Goodness knows why?

I was in the hospital for three weeks altogether. Some of my shipmates used to come and see me until they sailed again. My pay was brought to me and I signed off the ship. Len left the hospital a week before me but he and his wife Eva used to still come back and see me. One day Len asked me what I would do when I left hospital. I told him I would get a passage home as a Distressed British Seaman. He then asked me if I would like to come and stay with them for a couple of weeks while I recuperated. It sounded like a good offer so I was pleased to accept.

When it was time for me to leave, Len and Eva collected me in their car. It was an old 'Swift' open tourer. It had the throttle on the steering column and long running boards along the outside. The handbrake lever was outside the drivers door, as was the spare tyre. However, it drove very well and we were to have many Sunday outings in the Bush collecting firewood and shooting rabbits.

We arrived at their new three bedroom bungalow in Belmont, a suburb on the edge of town. It was a superb bungalow with large rooms and a garage. I was amazed to learn that, not only had they built it themselves, but had made every brick on site in single cavity moulds. They then advised me that they were going away on two weeks holiday the next day and would I mind if they left me alone to look after the bungalow. Again, I was amazed that they trusted a complete stranger to be in charge of their new home! They had stocked it up with food and hoped I would not mind them going. I had my pay from the Sedgepool so was alright for money.

While they were away I took the opportunity to have a good look around Geelong. There was a good tram service from the top of the road into town. I liked what I saw of the place. It was a medium sized town, about the size of Dover I suppose. Very nicely terraced gardens led down to the beach where a large circular fence of iron railings enclosed a good sized swimming area safe from sharks. These gardens etc. had been built by local labour during the interwar depression years. People had to EARN their dole money in Australia!

The Ford Motor Company had a large factory here and were the main employer. Len worked for them as a Panel Beater. The International Harvester Company also had a large plant building tractors and farm machinery. Geelongs main claim to notoriety though came from the wool industry. The two largest wool brokers were Dalgety & Co. and Elder, Smith & Co. both of whom owned a diversity of company's around the world, particularly in the U.K.

As I said earlier, I liked the look of Geelong. It had a nice 'feel' about it which was more than enhanced by the good friendship and trust I had found as soon as I got here. I soon decided it might be nice to stay here for a while. Say about 6 months. I went down to the Immigration office and told them of my desire. They just said "Welcome to Geelong" and stamped my pass there and then as an immigrant.

The next thing was to get a job. I thought I might as well utilise my time and learn something about the wool industry. Elder, Smiths were the largest wool brokers so I just walked in the door and enquired if there were any vacancies. The office manager came out to see me and, apparently finding me to be literate, immediately offered me a job as a 'Tally Clerk'.

It was the busiest time of the year in the wool industry. Clips were arriving in thick and fast from the sheep stations, some as far away as New South Wales. They valued the Geelong name tag for the processing of their fleeces. Some of the clips were so large that they spread out among other brokers. My job was to check the bales in and log where they had come from. Porters would truck the bales in and put them on the scales in front of me before taking them on to the processing rooms where they were checked and graded for quality. An average bale weighed 350 lbs and contained 30 fleeces. The average price paid at the International Auctions at that time was £3 a lb. The finest Merinos fetching £5 a lb. This was big money and boom time for the 'Cockies' as sheep farmers were known. At the end of the day we always had small brown paper bags of wool come in. These were the sheep rubbings on the barb wire fences that children, and grown ups, used to collect and send in. They used to get 10/- a lb for these. A useful little earner for the children!

It was not long before I found myself doing the Clerical work at the International Auction Rooms. I found it very interesting. The Russians and Japanese were very prominent buyers at the time. The Russians in particular seemed to force the prices up as they bought wool for their Military uniform requirements.

Len & Eva McKiernan at 2, Elizabeth St. Belmont, Geelong.
Opposite – the bungalow they built and where I stayed for nearly 3 years.

I had only been here a week when I saw that a dance was being held on the Saturday evening so I thought I would go. I found most of the girls were rather short for my 6'2" height but I spotted one who stood out above the others. I asked her for a dance and we finished up spending the evening together. Her name was Mary Atkin and she was the Art Teacher at the famous Geelong Technical College. Her widowed mother on a sheep station at a small village called Newstead about 120 miles away. Her married brother had a house on the station and ran the whole show. There was little Mary could out there so she had utilised her talents and trained to become a teacher. She also had lodgings in Geelong. We got along very well and made a date to meet again the next day.

Sheep farmers were making very good money at that time and when my colleagues at work heard of my date with Mary they ribbed me mercilessly. They said they had been looking for a ' Cockies' daughter all their lives and here was me, a mere 'Pommy', finding one the first week I was here!

When Len and Eva returned from their holiday they were more than surprised to find me ensconced in a job and with a girl friend, plus my decision to stay in Geelong for a while. A few days later they both said, "Lofty, we have been thinking things over and wondered whether you would like to lodge with us permanently while you are here?" I was delighted and we came to an arrangement over finances. It would be nearly 3 years before I finally left them.

It was November by now and Mary, although having known me about a month, asked me if I would like to go home to their farm for Christmas. I asked her if she shouldn't ask her Mother first ? "No, it will be quite alright she said". But I insisted and of course her Mother said it would be fine. Meanwhile Len and Eva were very good and invited her round for tea one Sunday. They told her she was welcome to come round whenever she liked. They were very pleased I had found such a good friend so soon. These were very happy days and I felt I had 'found my destiny' out here.

A couple of days before Christmas I boarded the train for the old Gold Mining town of Ballarat about 60 miles from Geelong. Mary had gone home earlier when College broke up. It was arranged that she and her Brother would meet me off the train in Ballarat and take me the 60 odd miles to their farm in their car. Meanwhile they had spent the day shopping in Ballarat. There were no shops anywhere near their farm in Newstead. I later found out that they virtually lived on lamb or mutton which they killed themselves. They grew their own vegetables and kept a dozen cows for milk, making their own butter, and had quite a few chickens which kept them supplied with eggs.

In hindsight I find it rather amusing that, when I boarded the train I was unaware they had 'Ladies Only' coaches out here. I entered one with three ladies sitting in it. They never said a word. It was only a little while after the train had started that I noticed a 'Ladies Only' sticker on the window. I immediately apologised and rose to leave by the corridor. One of them said "You are from the old country, aren't you?" I said "Yes". "Then don't leave they all said. We would love to hear what things are like in England these days". They insisted I stay and I kept them interested in relating my wartime and sea going experiences for the rest of the journey. It passed the time away for all of us and they were very profuse with their thanks for making it such an interesting journey.

Mary and her brother Douglas, together with his wife and two young children were waiting for me at the station. Fortunately they had a large American Pontiac car and there was plenty of room for all of us. During the journey home we had a puncture but Douglas soon changed the wheel.

When we arrived at the farm I found a large wooden farmhouse with corrugated iron roof which had been built by Mary's Grandfather. There were many out buildings and the whole was typical of the structures built in Victorian times in this part of the world.

As the car pulled up about a dozen mongrel dogs came charging up barking their heads off and jumping about all over the place. The dogs had lived in the farmyard all their lives and were never let into the house. Douglas had to get out of the car and quieten them down before the rest of us could get out. He picked up a stick to threaten them with and together with his shouting, they finally got the message and cringed away giving low growls and yelps.

Mary's mother came out to greet us and made me feel very welcome. She must have been a little apprehensive to meet her daughters 'Pommy Sailor Friend!'

The house, furniture and contents were all very Victorian. Like most country houses in Australia they possessed a Pianola which was their sole entertainment before the advent of the gramaphone and wireless. There was no electricity out there so oil lamps and candles were the only form of lighting. A wide porch ran around the outside of the house so the roof extended out over that. It kept the sun from shining in the windows and the house a bit cooler in the summer, but also made it rather dark inside during the day.

Mary showed me to my room, again very Victorian. A marble topped wash stand held a large decorative china bowl and jug of water. The large double bed had a feather mattress which, together with sheets and blankets, I found to be very comfortable but extremely hot at night. It was midsummer at Christmas don't forget!

I had a cold wash, changed my shirt and went in for dinner. The whole family joined us and we had the inevitable Lamb. Douglas killed their sheep as they wanted them and as far as I could see they ate no other meat. Mary told me that very occasionally they had the slaughterhouse kill a cow for them and keep it in their deep freeze. This was in Castlemaine about 30 miles away. It was the nearest town of any size and well known in England for its xxxx beer.

After dinner we chatted for a bit. They were interested to know my history and me theirs. Douglas soon took the children home to bed though and this was the signal for Mrs. Atkin to retire also. I noted she told Mary not to stay up too long, and got the feeling she thought we might be sitting and doing 'a bit of courting' until the early hours!

I had a bad night. It was terribly hot on that feather mattress. The noise of the Possums scratching around on the corrugated iron roof did nothing to help me sleep. I was glad when dawn broke and hoped it would not be long until Mary and her mother appeared on the scene. I eventually heard noises of some one up and about but it was still very early so I lay in bed a while longer until I thought it prudent to get up. I must have fallen asleep again because the next thing I knew was Mary bringing me in a cup of tea. "Had a good night?" she said. I thought it easier to say yes rather than try to explain why I had been awake most of the night!

Having finished my tea, I was about to get up when Mary came in again. this time with a jug of hot water for me to wash and shave. I was just wondering how I would go about my ablutions I told her. I was not used to these DIY plumbing systems!

Once washed and dressed in the appropriate shorts and shirt for such hot weather, I crept out to the kitchen to see if any breakfast was being made. It was, and Mary was the cook. I enquired where her Mother was and was told she had been up ages and was out in the dairy making butter and cream.

After breakfast Mary said "Why don't you go out for a little walk? I have some chores to do and Mother needs a hand". I saw a small hill not too far away and said I would go up there and take a look at my surroundings. "Don't go any further "said Mary. " It is very easy to get lost in the 'bush' round here!" "O.K." I said, and wandered off.

Most of the farmyard dogs followed me. I liked walking with dogs so was pleased to have their company. We got to the top of the hill and I surveyed the surrounding countryside which stretched for miles without a house in sight. Nothing but the bush and sheep all around me. The ground was grey with not a blade of grass to be seen. The soil would run through your fingers like silver sand. I later asked Douglas how the sheep survived. "We are in a drought situation at the moment" he said. "We are feeding the sheep with what is left of last years silage". I commented that I thought grass could never grow on that land again! In fact it looked as though it never had. "You would be surprised" he remarked. One good shower of rain and it all comes through again". A few days later it did. I found it hard to believe!

Getting back to my walk. There were quite a few trees about. A lot of them looked pretty dead but some were a good shade of green. It wasn't until I suddenly saw one tree suddenly lose all its greenery that I realised there had been hundreds of Budgerigars sitting on its bare branches and they had just taken off. An amazing sight!

I carried on walking for a while until I suddenly realised the dogs were no longer with me! On looking around I also realised I was not too sure which way to get back! Eventually I realised I was 'bushed'. Mary had warned me and now I knew how easy it was! Before long I was fortunate enough to come to a road. I thought, if I follow this I am bound to come to some habitation sooner or later! It must have been about 2 p.m. when I came across what was not much more than a shack. I was sweating freely in the 110 degrees plus temperature and feeling pretty well exhausted by this time. The 'shack' turned out to be a bar with a few men quenching their thirst inside. They all stopped talking (and drinking) when they saw a stranger walk in.

I asked if anyone could tell me the way to the Atkins farm at Newstead? "You mean to say you walked from there?" someone said. "Gor' blimey, only a stupid Pommy would do such a thing on a day like this". I had walked further than I thought. There was a wooden box telephone on the wall behind the bar. You had to wind the handle to get through to the operator. The barman phoned through to Douglas to say where I was. "The bloke looks pretty well 'tuckered'" I heard him say, " so I suggest you come and fetch him". That being done I was treated to 'one on the house' and told to watch what I was doing out here in the future.

Douglas soon arrived and said they were getting very worried about me and, when the dogs came back without me they thought some mishap might have occurred and were about to get a search party going. Mary was more than pleased to see I was alright. We had something to eat and then it was suggested we go for a swim. "A swim?" I said "Where on earth can you go for a swim around here?" "We will show you" said Mary. We all climbed into the farms Utility truck and Douglas drove us into the bush for about a mile until I suddenly saw a large reservoir. It was about the size of two football pitches. Mary's grandfather had built a dam across a small depression soon after he built the farm. There was an underground spring that kept the dam topped up even in times of drought. We just stripped own to our underwear and dived in. It was beautiful. What I thought to be some stones on the bottom turned out to be fresh water mussels there, hundreds of them and they were apparently good to eat, although I never tried any.

We went home for a traditional Christmas dinner of Turkey etc. but I found it very difficult to get into the spirit of Christmas when we were sweltering in temperatures of 110 degrees plus!

On Boxing Day, Mary suggested we go to see the Highland games in Castlemaine. We drove over in the Pontiac. It was very similar to Balmoral in Scotland. So many men in kilts, and a variety of tartans. Pipe bands from a wide area had come to compete in playing and marching skills. Nearly every town in Australia had its own Pipe Band. There was tossing the Caber, throwing the Haggis, Sword Dancing and many other sporting events such as sheep sheering and chopping thick logs in the shortest time. Many beer tents were in evidence and seemed to be doing a roaring trade. It was a great day out.

My visit to Newstead was short lived. I was due back at work the day after Boxing Day but decided I would take another day off. For a start the trains were not running and I also felt I had not spent a long enough time with Mary.

Mary had another three weeks off before going back to College but decided that, as there was nothing for her to do in Newstead, she would rather come back to Geelong with me. This pleased me no end as I was really beginning to enjoy her company. Her mother no doubt, was not so pleased at her early return!

Douglas drove us the 60 miles to Ballarat early next morning. Mary said it would be a good opportunity for me to visit the old Sovereign Hill goldmine which was now a museum. Ballarat was the centre of the great Australian Gold Rush in the 1800's. An area where fortunes were made, and lost!

The main digging area on Sovereign Hill had been turned into a really marvellous working museum. Workings, diggings, shops etc. have been rebuilt and reproduced exactly as they were in the old days, including wax models of people in the dress of that age. Guides and staff were also dressed in the old style thus creating an authentic scene of those days.

There are still small amounts of alluvial gold deposits in the stream that runs through the site and, by purchasing a Miners Licence for £2 you can do a bit of 'panning' yourself. I did this later on in 1975 when on a return visit there. I actually panned a small quantity of gold dust which was put into a small bottle of water for me to take home. The bottom of the bottle was black so it was easy to see the gold dust. We spent most of the day at Sovereign Hill before having a quick look around the town and getting the train back to Geelong.

I turned up at work the next day and made my apologies for my absence. These were rather grudgingly accepted I thought! In those days, in Australia at least, the days between Christmas and New Year were working days.

I had settled down to life and work in Geelong very well. I liked the people I met and those I worked with. I liked the Australian rough and ready, down to earth style. If a chap did not like you, he would come straight out and tell you even if he was only half your size. You knew where you were with people! I got on with Len and Eva most of all. I was beginning to think my future lay not only in Australia but with Mary! I gave serious thought to settling permanently in Geelong and even wrote to mother telling her to pack her bags and get out here.

Work was pretty hectic, but interesting and enjoyable none the less. Most evenings I spent with Mary. We led quite a simple life walking in the beautiful gardens or sitting on the sea front. The Saturday night dance was always enjoyable. On Wednesday evenings there was always Old Time Dancing and Square Dancing at which they used to show all the old time silent movies on a screen at one end of the dance hall. That was always good fun.

Weekends always seemed to run to a pattern. I worked Saturday mornings. In the afternoon I took my weekly bath. The reason it was weekly was because there was no gas in Geelong and most people had 'Chip Heaters' for the hot water. These were like our old pre-war cylindrical Geysers over one end of the bath, but instead of a gas heater under them you used firewood. If you wanted a bath you had to go out into the back garden, chop a load of firewood up and keep the fire going while running the bath. The slower you ran the water the hotter it was. Len & Eva always had theirs on Sunday so it was Saturday for me.

Most Sunday mornings, Len and I would go out into the 'bush' in his old Swift convertible. We had two objectives. One to collect firewood for our weekly baths and the other to shoot rabbits. I had bought a .22 rifle similar to Lens and we would shoot as many as 140 between us on a good day. They seemed to sit around in groups of hundreds, you could hardly miss them. It was also a very profitable day out. We got a shilling for the rabbit and 4d. for the pelt. A good days income at that time. Meat rationing was still on in England so there was a ready export for them.

Mary sometimes came out with us which was very handy as she would cook lunch. This was always a very simple affair. We would take some large rump steaks out with us and a ¼" thick square steel plate, two piles of earth were made across which we would lay the plate. We lit a wood fire under it and in no time at all we had some beautiful steaks sizzling away on top. We never bothered to have anything else with them, but tea brewed in a Billy can over a wood fire tasted marvellous. A good steak and a Billy can of tea in the outback of Australia is something I will always relish the memory of.

If Mary did not come with us, she would sometimes go round and help Eva who in traditional Australian style, did the weeks baking on a Sunday. Cakes, pastry, bread and pies would be made for the whole week. I made a big faux pas the first time I had Sunday tea with them, she used to display her days baking on the table. Not knowing it was the weeks bake, I dug mercilessly into it. They said nothing, but a few days later I discovered this habit during a normal conversation. I felt awful and apologised for my greed of last week which they accepted with a laugh. I never lived it down though!

As time went on I was introduced to all Len & Eva's friends. I was always invited round when they were and often on my own. It was noticeable that there was little or no crime there at the time. No one thought of locking their doors! Friends and neighbours would just barge in with a Coo-ee.

Life had settled in to pretty much of a routine for about 18 months. I did not realise it but apparently, and quite unconsciously, I had acquired a broad

Australian accent. So much so that even the locals would not believe I was a 'Pommy'.

By now Mary and I had an 'understanding' that we would eventually get married. I had nothing to offer her at the time and it would take quite a while of hard saving to achieve this. I certainly felt I belonged in Geelong and saw my future here.

One day, one of the acquaintances I had made, Jack Roberts the Harbour Master, asked me if I would be interested in joining the Geelong Harbour Trust. Jack was an old Mancunian who had been out here a number of years. The Trust had two large American built Diesel Electric tugs which were fine looking vessels. They were kept continually at work docking and undocking ships, towing barges up to Melbourne and could go out into the Bass Strait if any ship needed assistance. This notoriously dangerous strait had fast tide rips and more often than not rough weather.

The Captains of both tugs were nearing retiring age and Jack, knowing I was an old deep sea tug man, albeit in the engine room, thought that if I joined them as a mate, I could study for my Home Trade ticket and might eventually be able to take over as Captain. This sounded like a great opportunity to me. I was beginning to get a bit bored with the indoor life at the wool brokers and what was more, the pay would be substantially more! Shipboard life would be mine again! I accepted immediately. There would be a lot to learn and a busier life than I ever imagined was to follow. I was still young though and had a good capacity for learning.

Geelong was situated in Corio Bay which is a large bay in itself within the much larger Port Phillip Bay leading up to Melbourne. The Shell Oil Company were about to build a large Oil Refinery here. There would be even more work for the tugs once the huge oil tankers started to arrive. The future looked quite exciting and secure. I needed to get two years local experience as Mate before I could even sit for my home trade ticket. That should give me plenty of time to study and learn the job.

CHAPTER TWELVE

ss.Clintonia (Stag Line of Newcastle)

I had been working for the Geelong Harbour Trust for about 14 months and was certainly enjoying the life and anticipating a bright future when suddenly the course of my life was changed yet again. I was walking down the main street one day and could not believe my eyes. I bumped into an old war time shipmate in the form of Bill Rush who was now 2nd. Mate on the Clintonia, a ship I had helped to dock a couple of days ago. She was in need of some repairs and expected to be here about two weeks before loading a cargo of grain for the U.K. We had a quick chat and arranged to meet in the evening.

I introduced him to Mary and she soon found a friend to make up a foursome while he was here. This is where fate took a hand once again in the future course of my life. We enjoyed a couple of weeks during Bills stay here and then, a couple of days before he was due to sail, he told me their 5th. Engineer had gone into the same hospital I was in and they would be sailing without him in two days time. I must confess I felt a little envious of him sailing home , in spite of my new found fortunes in Australia. Bill said " Do you fancy a trip home. We will be back here again in 3 months?" Now here was something that required some quick thought! I had left home over 3 years ago for a 6 month round the world voyage. Here was an opportunity to go home for a visit and get paid for the round trip. I could make arrangements for mother to come out and at least help out with her fare. My mind was in a turmoil. Mary chipped in "Go while you have the chance" she said. Len and Eva said likewise. But what about my job, I thought! I saw Jack Roberts first thing in the morning. I explained the situation to him and asked if it would be possible for me to take 3 months 'leave of absence'. Both he and the Board of Directors were very understanding about it and said "Go with our blessing and your job will be waiting for you when you get back", or words to that effect.

Having cleared myself ashore I went on board to see the Chief Engineer. He said he would be pleased to have me. I suppose it was me or they would have to sail without a fifth engineer. I then went to the local Customs & Immigration to appraise them of my intentions. I was told I could not leave the country without a clearance from the Income Tax authorities. That was 50 miles away in Melbourne and we were sailing tomorrow! The Customs were very helpful, they phoned the Melbourne Office explaining the situation. They in turn said that, if I could get to Melbourne and sign a declaration form that day they would sort it out. I took a Taxi to Melbourne. He waited about 20 minutes for me while I was in the office. I not only got my clearance in that time but a £22 rebate. He then drove me back to Geelong. The fare was an unbelievable £5! Could you imagine all that happening in England ?

I went back to Len and Eva's and packed all my gear and boarded the 'Clintonia' that evening. I went ashore again to say my farewells. Mary was a bit tearful and apprehensive I thought! However, she said how happy she was for me and looked forward to my return. We sailed the next morning. There were about thirty people down on the jetty to see me off. I had not known anyone when I arrived in Australia! I am sure the Clintonia had never had such a send off since the day of her launch.

The trip home proved to be not only horrendous, but frightening and I rue the day I ever joined the ship. To start with it was extremely rough as soon as we cleared Port Phillip Heads and turned into the Bass Strait. In fact it was very rough all the way across the Great Australian Bight. The main and only interest was the large Albatross that accompanied us for 3-4 days. It never seemed to flap its wings but always rose and dropped to the contours of the waves as it gracefully soared along. We were pleased when we had crossed the Bight and headed in a more northerly direction where we could expect some better weather. We called in at Freemantle for bunkers and managed to get a run ashore for a look around.

I made good use of Bill Rush on the way home. He knew of my intentions to sit for my Home Trade ticket in Geelong and taught me many things I might need to know. He also schooled me in Navigation and I soon learned out how to work out the ships daily run and position, and how to use Nicholsons Tables and Logarithms. There were no Satellite Navigational Systems in those days. It took two foolscap sheets of pure maths to do it.

Bill was amazed at my adeptness and said "Why don't you go for your deep sea ticket while you are about it?" I gave that idea a lot of thought! The 'horrendous' part of the voyage started when we were half way across the Indian Ocean. We had many fire tubes start leaking in the back end of the boilers. That meant they would have to be expanded to stop the leaks. A lousy enough job in port with the boilers cold, but at sea, with the boilers full of steam!!! We had to stop the engine and lower the steam pressure for starters. The furnaces were turned off, wooden planks were placed down their length. We engineers and the Donkeyman then wrapped ourselves in as many old clothes as we could, wound sacking round ourselves then tied a rope round our waists. Having done all that we crawled with great difficulty into the back ends. Once in you could stand upright, locate the leaky tubes with the aid of a torch, insert an expending mandrill and pull down with all your might on a ratchet spanner.

By now you could hardly breathe at all and the sweat was just rolling out of you. Your aim was to try and expend one tube in less than a minute then get out as fast as you could with those on the outside pulling on your rope. Each of the 48 tubes in each furnace had to be done in turn and there were three furnaces to each of the two boilers. We just drifted engineless in the Indian Ocean for two days while doing this, and everyone was exhausted and dehydrated after we had finished. Goodness knows how much weight I lost. Reminiscent of my days in the Tug Assiduous and not so far away from where I was then either!

We eventually got away again. Up through the Red Sea, Suez Canal and Mediterranean where we were pleased to get into some cooler weather. Once we were through the Straits of Gibraltar we felt we were almost home . All was not over yet though. As we approached the English Channel with thoughts of our imminent arrival in Newcastle in a couple of days, we had ' panic stations' in the boiler room once again. The crowns of the actual furnaces were spraying steam into the flames. Then we noticed the circular furnace drums flattening out at the top. They had worn thin over the years and were starting to collapse as well as being perforated. We had to reduce steam pressure and therefore speed immediately. It was thought we should go into nearby Falmouth but the owners wanted her back in her home port of Newcastle if at all possible. They were not sailing on this time bomb! The Chief agreed to give it a try. We made it, under continual apprehension all the way. It took us another 4 days instead of 2 to get there. We were lucky to have made it at all!

Now my big problem arose! There was no way this ship was going back to Australia again and, even if they put new boilers in her, there was no way I would ever sail on her again. I had more than enough of that poorly maintained ship.

I was more than pleased to sign off her and get down to Brighton to see mother again after nearly 4 years away. She, of course, was pleased to see me.

I was not to know the Clintonia was in such bad shape otherwise I would certainly not have joined her. My meeting with Bill Rush had certainly changed the course of my life again. I could not afford the passage back to Australia and took a job ashore in Brighton. It was to be the end of my sea going career.

I eventually met and married my first wife, Olive Edwards, and never went back to Australia again apart from going on a Trade Mission for my company in 1975. I had lost touch with everyone out there, including Mary.

While spending a week in Melbourne for the engineering exhibition in 1975, I took the opportunity to visit Geelong at the weekend. I went to the bungalow to see if Len and Eva were still there. Eva opened the door to my ring and immediately said "Christ almighty if it ain't Lofty" and this after nearly 30 years! I stayed a couple of nights with them and met their 4 grown up boys. They had no children when I left them. We had a whale of a weekend.

I often wonder where I would be today if I had gone back! But then…my children and grandchildren would never have been born let alone be in a position to read this story!

Life is full of 'Why's', 'Wherefores' and 'Ifs' and 'Buts' isn't it? Having reached the end of my story I am very pleased to have finally written it. It means there is at least a record that I existed on this earth, otherwise it would not be many years before, like me, who knows nothing about my own father's or grandfather's life my own offspring might have wondered what I did in my early years!

THE END